Shilpa

Julie Aspinall

Shilpa

The Biography

JB

JOHN BLAKE

Published by John Blake Publishing Ltd,
3 Bramber Court, 2 Bramber Road,
London W14 9PB, England

www.blake.co.uk

First published in paperback in 2007

ISBN: 978 1 84454 467 7

British Library Cataloguing-in-Publication Data:

A catalogue record for this book is available from the British Library.

Design by www.envydesign.co.uk

Printed in the UK by CPI Bookmarque, Croydon, CR0 4TD

1 3 5 7 9 10 8 6 4 2

Contents

1

Beauty and the Bigots

The world watched aghast. On the television screen, two young women were pitted against one another: one, a tall, slim Indian woman in her early thirties, her face a picture of disbelief; the other, shorter, dumpier and younger, had her face twisted into an animal-like snarl. 'Your head's so far up your arse you can smell your own shit!' she hissed, utterly unaware of how she was coming across to her fellow housemates, the television audience and, most damagingly of all perhaps, the outside world.

For this was the culmination of days of bullying, aggressive behaviour from Jade Goody, Danielle Lloyd and Jo O'Meara, three housemates on *Celebrity Big*

Brother, broadcast in January 2007, towards the beautiful Indian actress in their midst, Shilpa Shetty. The three of them sounded like fishwives – and that is the charitable view – shrieking out racist abuse, clearly beside themselves with jealousy directed at the woman who was everything they were not.

Concern – and fury – had been mounting for days now at what seemed like a display of racial hatred developing on their television screens. Not only did Jade seem to be about to destroy herself but it also looked as if the abuse was on the verge of causing a diplomatic incident. On a visit to India, Chancellor Gordon Brown was clearly livid. Commenting on the furore, he hoped the message that 'we are a nation of fairness and tolerance' came across and added for good measure that the bullying was 'offensive'.

In fact, the timing of Mr Brown's visit to the subcontinent couldn't have been worse. While clearly wanting to pontificate on matters of international politics, he was not allowed to get away from the only subject everyone was interested in. 'I understand that in the UK there have already been 10,000 complaints from viewers about these remarks which people see, rightly, as offensive,' he said. (In fact, the complaints were ultimately to top 40,000.) 'I want Britain to be seen as a country of fairness and tolerance. Anything detracting from this I condemn.'

It was quite incredible that matters had come to this. Politicians from both Britain and India had got involved: Treasury Minister Ed Balls said he was 'ashamed' of what had happened and that 'the image it projects of Britain around the world is appalling'. It certainly was. Demonstrators had taken to the streets in India, burning an effigy of the makers of *Big Brother* and carrying banners that read: 'Death to Big Brother' and 'Do not treat our Shilpa unfairly'. The Indian Junior Foreign Minister Anand Sharm announced there would be a formal complaint, adding, 'Racism has no place in a civilised society.'

But it was only too evident in the *Big Brother* household. For several days now, the three women, with Jade's boyfriend Jack, had been making Shilpa's life a misery. She had been described as a dog and told to pick chicken bones out of the lavatory with her teeth. Jade's mother asked her if she lived in a shack; she had been derisively referred to as the 'Indian'; there was speculation as to whether she ate with her hands and, after preparing food, she had been insulted by Danielle commenting that you didn't know 'where those hands have been'. All this was directed at one of the most famous actresses in Bollywood – it was a stomach-turning spectacle and one which showed no signs of coming to a halt.

And it had all begun with a most unlikely cause – a chicken. Shilpa had been roasting a chicken, which turned out to be underdone, prompting a barrage of insults from her housemates, who had already shown signs of being extremely prickly towards her. Much has been made of their racist slurs, but it was clear that what really lay behind the problem was that old British chestnut: class. Shilpa was classy, well educated and, what seemed to be a particular bone of contention, had servants – quite a lot of them, in fact. None of the girls baiting her, along with Jack, seemed able to bear this. Jo remarked that people in India must be slim because their food made them ill, being always undercooked. 'I don't trust that chicken,' she said. 'I want to eat it but I'm scared.' Danielle, who had previously distinguished herself by referring to Winston Churchill as the first black American president, commented, 'I love Indian food, but I think it probably tastes better in the UK. Is that right?' Other comments included, 'They eat with their hands in India, don't they – or is that China? You don't know where those hands have been.'

What was probably the case – and the girls in their

dim way sensed this – was that Shilpa was not used to cooking as she had always had servants to do it all for her and therefore was not sure about the way a chicken should be cooked. But such was the furore created by the episode that her mother felt compelled to defend her afterwards. 'You know, I microwave a meal in 15 minutes and that includes the spicy masalas,' she said. 'Did they not have a microwave in that place? That is how we cook in our home and Shilpa is used to doing it that way. She should have left it to them to prepare their meals.'

Certainly, Jade's venom seemed to be getting worse by the minute. 'She's apparently some Bollywood actress, but I've never heard of her,' she snarled. 'For all I know, she could be someone off the Old Kent Road. I've seen how she goes in and out of people's arseholes; I've seen her whispering, laughing, behind each other's backs! She is fucking sly. I wouldn't trust her as far as I could throw her! She isn't genuine.'

Not to be outdone, her boyfriend Jack added, 'We should lock the door and put her out in the garden.'

It was unbelievable that matters had been allowed to get this far. When Shilpa had been bleaching her facial hair, Danielle asked, 'Do you get stubble?' She later added, 'She wants to be white. She's a dog.'

Of course, Shilpa, who easily outshone every other woman present, was anything but, as Danielle was well aware. But her vindictiveness and jealousy were driving her to further extremes, which got nastier as the show went on.

Jade, certainly, seemed to be quite obsessed with Shilpa's background. During a row about an Oxo cube, which escalated totally out of proportion to the actual subject matter, she became hysterical. 'You're a fucking loser and a liar; you need a day in the slums!' she screeched. 'Shut the fuck up! Who the fuck are you? You aren't some princess in Neverland, you're a normal housemate like everyone else!' She also referred to her as 'Shilpa Fuckawallah', 'Shilpa Durupa' and 'Shilpa Poppadom'.

Indeed, at some points, matters almost became surreal. Jade said, 'She makes me feel sick. She makes my skin crawl.'

Later, it was far worse when Jack said, 'I don't like her. In fact, I hate her. She came into this house … fucking ****!' There was intense speculation he'd used the word 'Paki'; Channel 4 insisted that it was all right really, as he'd actually used the word, c**t! That the situation should have descended to a level where this insult was actually revealed to reassure viewers about the level of abuse Shilpa was enduring was enough to show quite how far things had got out of hand.

Matters continued to worsen. Up until then, the bosses at the station had said nothing publicly, contenting themselves with putting out a statement which read, 'Matters of bullying or racial abuse in any form are taken extremely seriously by Channel 4. The nature of the show often includes incidents where conflicts arise and housemates are encouraged to resolve issues among themselves. Shetty herself has not voiced any concerns of racial slurs or bullying. The social interactions of the group are part of the *Big Brother* story and viewers have a right to see these portrayed.'

It was not enough. They were 'hiding behind a statement', said the Asian Labour MP for Leicester East Keith Vaz, urging them to put a stop to it there and then.

Prime Minister Tony Blair was dragged into it, too. 'I have not seen the programme in question, but I would agree entirely with the principle he [Vaz] has outlined, which is that we should oppose racism in all its forms.'

Not to be outdone, the Tories stepped in. 'It is quite wrong that the programme should tolerate racist abuse and behaviour from participants and I believe it is an issue that should be addressed immediately,' said Conservative spokesman Dominic Grieve.

Most damagingly still, from the point of view of the programme makers, Shilpa's mother Sunanda spoke of her distress. Shilpa had been reduced to tears on screen, which had not mollified her tormentors one bit, and had deeply upset everyone close to her. 'As a mother, I find it very painful and alarming to watch my daughter cry,' she said. 'To see her cry on TV while a bunch of people abuse her is very painful for a parent. I have never seen her cry, maybe when she's been heartbroken, but she's normally a very happy person.'

As if all this were not enough, the sponsor of the show, Carphone Warehouse, decided to withdraw its backing. Indeed, the company was at pains to emphasise its disgust at what had been going on and released a lengthy statement washing its hands of the whole proceedings.

'Our concern has rapidly mounted about the broadcast behaviour of individuals within the *Big Brother* house,' said the CEO of Carphone Warehouse, in a statement issued on 18 January 2007. 'We are totally against all forms of racism and bullying, and indeed this behaviour is entirely at odds with the brand values of the Carphone Warehouse. As a result, we feel that as long as this continues we are unable to associate our brand with the programme. We had already made it clear to Channel 4 that were this to continue we would have to consider our position. Nothing we saw last night gave us any comfort. Accordingly we have instructed Channel 4 to remove our sponsorship name and branding with immediate effect.'

Some were keen to point out that it is almost inconceivable that this should have happened if the victim had been someone who was disabled. 'They have made a rather bland statement about condemning racism of any kind,' said comedian Meera Syal of Channel 4. 'But I am just wondering if, on their last series, for example, the Tourette's sufferer had been called a "spaz" on a regular basis, whether they would have let that continue.'

Another Asian person who had been in the *Big Brother* household (albeit the non-celebrity version) held similar views. 'It's gone beyond that very thin line of what is racism and what isn't,' said Narinder Kaur. 'It is disgusting and I am quite flabbergasted that three grown women can sit there and be so ignorant.'

Finally, a decision was made to say something, but not only was it too little, too late, it was also a PR disaster for everyone concerned. To begin with, Channel 4 chairman Luke Johnson went on Radio 4's *Today* programme ostensibly to talk about the BBC licence-fee decision which was due to be announced later in the day. Of course, inevitably, he was asked about the uproar surrounding *Big Brother*. Only a series of 'no comments' was forthcoming, along with a repeated reference to the statement already put out by Channel 4. It was toe curling to listen to and, as commentators were quick to point out, he only had Greg Wood, the programme's business correspondent to deal with. Had the interrogator been John Humphrys, it was widely felt matters would have been made worse still.

Only a few hours later, Channel 4's chief executive Andy Duncan appeared at a press conference and, even though he clearly knew what to expect in the line of questioning, he could not rein in the furore. By now, the row had reached global proportions and images of him were being beamed all over the world.

Unlike that morning, there was no line of gentle questioning for him to attempt to brush aside: rather, he came under savage attack from a reporter from *Sky News*. He pointed out that a culture clash had been almost inevitable and that Shilpa had not complained of racism. But it was no good; the damage had already been done. Even after a reconciliation was staged between Jade and Shilpa, and the former evicted, questions were still being asked. Indeed, the board of Channel 4 held a meeting at which executives discussed the whole situation. The very future of the show was in doubt.

Nor were others prepared to let the matter drop. Teenagers should be taught 'British values' to combat racist and ignorant attitudes, according to the Education Secretary Alan Johnson, who added, 'The current debate has highlighted the need to make sure schools focus on the core British values of justice and tolerance. We want the world to be talking about the respect and understanding we give all cultures, not the ignorance and bigotry shown on our TV screens.'

Trevor Phillips, chairman of the Commission for Equality and Human Rights, said Luke Johnson should be censured, too. 'There is no question that if the Channel 4 board does not say that Johnson was wrong not to talk about it last week, that his executives were wrong to say that there was no racism involved … if the board does not take that stand then I think Tessa Jowell has to step in and ask if this is a board that is capable of holding a public asset in trust for us,' he commented. 'I think it is that serious.'

When it finally came, the end was provided by the person who had started it all: Jade. Equally desperate not to break their own rules by intervening, yet watching in horror as their most famous housemate destroyed herself on live television, Channel 4 can only have been relieved when it finally emerged that the two people up for eviction were Shilpa and Jade. As the bosses knew it would be, this vote was immediately turned into a referendum on racism: would viewers support 'racist' Jade or her victim Shilpa? In the event, 82 per cent of the vote voted for Shilpa, with a very chastened Jade being booted out of the house. Belatedly, she began to take on the full implications of what she had done.

Indeed, after a Big Brother briefing, only a bit of which was televised, Jade's attitude seemed to change dramatically. In a bid to make up, she hugged Shilpa and expressed regret if her actions and opinions had offended any Indians. Channel 4, meanwhile, was doing everything it could to defuse matters: there would be no baying crowd waiting for Jade's release, just a quiet interview with Davina McCall. Jade herself pretty much gave the game away that she'd been warned what damage her actions had done when the result of the vote was announced. Unusually, there was no screaming from outside. 'I know why there's no noise,' she said.

'Why?' asked Shilpa.

'I know, but I can't tell you,' she replied.

Shilpa showed a great deal more forgiveness than she might have done, even expressing concern for Jade on the outside. 'I didn't want her to go with no one liking her,' she said. 'I hope she's OK.'

It was evident on her exit that Jade was now horribly aware of what she'd done to herself. Davina showed clips of her ranting like a fishwife: 'I'm disgusted with myself,' she said, as well she might be. 'I don't judge people by the colour of their skin.' Indeed, she looked pretty petrified. 'I don't want to be hated,' she said. 'Before, I didn't have anything to lose, and now I have so much ... I'll be going because people will think I'm a racist bitch and I'm not. I'm so scared – I've never been so scared in my life. The whole feeling of being rejected absolutely kills me.'

This, then, is the conclusion to the great *Big Brother* experiment: take someone from nowhere, elevate her to the heights of fame and then see her self-destruct. Jade might have had a good deal to apologise for, but she was not alone. How had the situation got out of hand? It was not an edifying sight.

Inside the house, Shilpa said she thought the bullying was not racist; outside, meanwhile, Jade was dropped as the face of an anti-bullying campaign, while Debenhams and The Perfume Shop withdrew her scent from sale. Shortly afterwards, it was announced that the paperback edition of her autobiography was not going to be published on the expected date. Despite her quite despicable behaviour, Jade became a figure to be pitied. She was as manipulated as everyone else. The creation of reality television, she was now being savaged by the beast that made her famous.

Danielle's career looked to be in equally dire straits, with urgent damage limitation going on outside. Angela de Fouw, her spokesperson, leaped to her client's defence. 'Danielle would be distraught to have been associated or linked with any form of alleged racism,' she said. 'Many of Danielle's closest friends are from multi-cultural backgrounds and are of diverse races. Danielle is the last person who would condone any form of racism or bullying.' But it was all too late.

Given the dignity and grace displayed by Shilpa within the house, it came as no surprise that her mother took an equally gracious view. 'I actually fear for Jade's safety,' she said. 'After the way she's behaved, I know there are a lot of angry people out to get her – and not just Shilpa's fans and fellow Indians. I'm getting calls from people all over the world, all colours and backgrounds who are disgusted by her comments. We are praying to God for Jade's wellbeing, spiritually and physically. I have no rancour in my heart for Jade. She's just an ignorant girl who knows very little about other people's cultures. It's sad, but I would not want to see anything bad happen.'

She was not, however, anything like as forgiving towards the programme makers, who she saw as putting Shilpa through an unforgivable ordeal. 'It is an ugly and vulgar show which has run its course,' she said. 'It must end with this one. There is already enough conflict in the world. We don't need to create it artificially and call it entertainment. This has been one of the most unpleasant events I have encountered on television. I don't mind some friction – it is inevitable when you create this kind of environment. But the show is deeply flawed. They should have provided firm guidelines from the start to ensure a level of respect for other people's culture. Instead, they turned it into a combat zone, which left my child exposed and vulnerable. Nobody warned us this could happen.'

No one had realised what could happen either and in time Sunanda was able to take reassurance from the fact that Shilpa was practically guaranteed a hero's welcome on her return to her home country (to say nothing of the fact that she was now world famous). 'It is already clear that she will be welcomed as a hero,' she said. 'Shilpa has always been adored here. She puts her fame in the country of her birth above everything. I want to march into the house and take her out. And if she leaves I will be there to hug her and tell her I love her.'

The message, as far as Jade was concerned, continued to be one of forgiveness. 'Shilpa is such a positive human being she always bounces back and she cannot have anything to do with negativity,' said her spokesman Dale Bhagwagar. 'She believes in moving on and not having negative thoughts, and when she gets out of the *Big Brother* house she will want to meet up with Jade and her mother Jackiey, go to their houses and show she does not hold any grudges. She is just as likely to invite Jade to India to see the country for herself. Shilpa is a very warm and spiritual person. If someone really hurt her, all she would do is ignore them and treat them as if they never existed.'

Sunanda also, rather understandably, wanted to question her daughter's tormentors. Whatever their motivation – racism, jealousy, class conflict – their behaviour reeked of the worst excesses of the school playground. Even allowing for the fact that Shilpa could come across as a mite high-handed, absolutely nothing could excuse their treatment of her, especially the way in which she, one person, was picked on by a gang that at times numbered five.

'What I'd like to ask the members of the family who have been abusing Shilpa is why?' she continued. 'They have acted like school bullies. If I meet either when I come to London, I'd say the same thing but I am not going to hunt them down. I have always brought my daughters up to be respectful of others. That's clearly not the case with Jade. The people who have racially abused Shilpa are jealous of her looks and are clearly ill educated. I don't believe these opinions reflect that of the British public. We have been to London dozens of times and are always treated well.'

Shilpa's father Surendra, 57, was also looking forward to seeing his daughter. 'We are both looking to travel to London next week,' he said.

Of course, the Shettys were not alone in their dismay at what had been done. Britain's entire political establishment, never slow to leap on a bandwagon, had already had their say, with real concerns in many quarters about how Britain came across to the outside world. But many were upset on a personal level, too. Film director Ken Russell, initially himself a housemate, who had been driven out by the sheer vulgarity of the Goodys, was horrified at what had been going on. 'Later, when her [Jade's] mother was ignominiously sent off, I thought things might improve,' he wrote. 'Not a bit of it. I watched, appalled, as Jade vented her wrath at the most sanguine person in the house – the divine Shilpa. Not only that, but Jade also impressed two cohorts to join her in the persecution.'

Jade by now was well and truly aware of what she'd done. A *mea culpa* world tour ensued, as she desperately tried to backtrack – very ironically, she herself is of mixed race as her paternal grandfather was black – apologising for her behaviour and voicing utter regret. A visit to India to apologise to the entire nation was planned, as she went from one television studio to the next in an effort to exonerate herself.

'No, I'm not a racist, but I accept I made racist comments,' she said in one no-holds barred interview with a Sunday newspaper. 'I don't see people for the colour that they are, or where they come from. I'm mixed race myself and I speak to everyone of every colour, background and nationality. I don't care about where people are from. I'm not going to justify my actions because they were wrong. I was shocked to see how I behaved. I was shocked and disgusted at myself.'

Indeed, she seemed absolutely determined to come up with every criticism of her own behaviour that she could think of before anyone else got the chance to say it for her. 'I don't know why I said those things to her or why those words came into my head,' she said. 'I wasn't thinking in my head a nasty thought. I'm not making excuses because I know that it's wrong. I now know that it's offensive. Maybe I'm just really stupid and nasty at heart, but I really don't think I am. My anger when I watched it on the screen shocked me. I didn't like it; I didn't know that my presence could be so intimidating or bullying.'

As a matter of fact, Jade did slightly understand the reason why she behaved in the way that she did, even though she had some difficulty enunciating it. Her background could not have been more different from Shilpa's, and it was clearly that, combined with jealousy, that provoked her in the way that it did. One of the sad things about the whole affair is the way she demeaned herself so much. In some ways, she had been an admirable figure up until then – she used the only means available to her, reality television, to haul herself up out of poverty and resolutely failed to blame the system that had deprived her. But now, she clearly saw that her background had come back to haunt her, and she might as well confront that head on.

'I've never blamed my past for anything I've done, but I don't know any other way,' she said (and what a condemnation of the way Britain has allowed an underclass to develop was there). 'My only way to argue is to shout – to get louder and louder so that I can't hear what they're saying. It's the way I am. I didn't know it was a problem until I watched it. I don't want people to be scared of me, or think that I'm intimidating. I hold my hand up to my comments and to people reading them or hearing them and thinking I'm a racist. I can understand why those words would look racist because I didn't get on particularly well with Shilpa. It's offensive to her and her culture. I didn't think "poppadom" was a racist word. I now know that things that I may not think are racist can actually be racist. It's my own fault for not knowing enough about other people's cultures.' Say what you like, Jade was certainly facing her own demons head on.

She realised something else, too – namely that she was a role model these days for some segments of the community and was expected to behave as such. Jade should probably never, ever have been put in a situation where she was allowed to become a role model, but that is what had happened and she was well aware of it herself. 'I feel shit,' she said. 'I hate myself right now. The first time I was on *Big Brother*, it was like a holiday camp but I've now got people out there who look up to me. I didn't want to get evicted for the wrong reasons. Evict me because I'm loud or annoying, but not because I'm a racist, because I'm not.'

Poor Jade – ultimately a woman to be pitied, as much as condemned. But she was, in many ways, yesterday's news. While her own drive to rehabilitate herself continued, it was Shilpa who was now the focus of attention all over the world, just as she had been for years in her native India. It was Shilpa who, having endured a very unpleasant experience, was ultimately going to emerge from the ordeal with dignity, grace and any number of advantageous career options now available to her. So just who is Shilpa Shetty – and how did she end up in the *Big Brother* household?

2
January 2007

Just a couple of weeks earlier, the world was intrigued when a slim and very striking Bollywood actress became the first-ever Indian star to enter the *Big Brother* house. A household name across Asia, Shilpa Shetty was almost entirely unknown in the West and initially, at least, not a great deal of information was forthcoming. Known to be 31, with a black belt in karate, and 'the best body in Bollywood', Shilpa came, quite literally, from a different world to that of everyone else present in the house. Above all, of course, was the contrast between Shilpa and the Goody clan that was not only going to electrify viewers, but also very nearly caused an international incident. Her beauty, intelligence, class and education highlighted only too well her new housemates' lack of all those qualities with explosive results.

But, back at the beginning, Shilpa had no idea what she was going to find in the house. Clad in a glamorous green sari, with full Bollywood make-up and jewellery, she waved at viewers as she made her way into the house, exotic as a peacock among the homegrown sparrows already in situ. 'I have zero expectations,' she said. 'The only thing I really hope is to keep my self-respect and my dignity.' She could have had no idea quite how severely the two were to be tested before her time in the house was up.

Given that Shilpa was clearly no ordinary housemate, it was no surprise that her contract was not that ordinary either. Negotiated under the firm eye of her mother Sunanda, who'd apparently had doubts about letting her daughter go into the house, it ensured Shilpa was being paid an estimated £357,000 to take part. Given the fact that standards of behaviour in the house were frequently on the low side, there were other clauses written into her contract, too: she would not wear a bikini, have to join the others in the pool or eat meat on Thursdays (in accordance with Hindu religion). Nor would she have to drink an excessive amount of alcohol or kiss anyone, men and women alike, on the lips. 'I had seen some extracts from a previous year and I knew it could get pretty raunchy,' said Sunanda. 'In one scene, I saw a young girl being egged on to drink alcohol until she was so drunk she fell out of the shower semi-naked in a very undignified way. I did not want Shilpa to be forced to do anything that would let her country down.'

Whatever Shilpa was bringing to the house, it was clearly going to be something pretty different from the exhibitionist drunken behaviour of past contestants. Ironically, her well-behaved and modest demeanour was to give rise to a good deal of soul searching on the outside about where British womanhood had gone wrong.

The world outside was certainly impressed. Shilpa was variously described as 'beautiful', 'graceful' and a 'lovely Indian lady'. Everyone was intrigued, too. Although she was known to be an actress, that was practically all British viewers knew about her and stories began to circulate about the style in which she lived; the exact level of her fame and what really lay behind her desire to enter the house. Davina McCall, as usual, was instigating the proceedings; she asked Shilpa what she hoped to achieve. 'I want to clear out the misconception of Indian people,' Shilpa replied. 'We are modern, intelligent and glamorous. I want all of India to be proud of me.'

She probably achieved that along with a great deal of Britain becoming rather ashamed of itself. At that stage, three of the housemates were missing – indeed, for several days no one would have a clue that they were going to turn up – but what Shilpa managed to do was present a face of India that was far more attractive than anything put forward by the West. Dignified, intelligent, sophisticated and, for want of a better word, classy, she soon proved herself to be everything the other housemates were not – with, as the world now knows, explosive results.

And, really, the biggest benefit to what was to turn into an ordeal was exposure to the West. Shilpa made no secret of her desire to act in Western films as well as Indian ones, and now was her chance to show herself off to both filmmakers and the audience who could take her career that one step ahead. The loud-mouthed comedian Russell Brand, who was hosting a spin-off show called *Big Brother's Big Mouth*, said as much: 'This is her chance to show herself to a Western audience,' he commented.

Not everyone, however, was impressed. For a start,

Shilpa's own parents were said to be hardly delighted about her decision to join the house. 'I did not want her to go,' said her mother, Sunanda. 'I have always travelled with her and this is the first time she has gone away to work without me there to protect her. She's a very spiritual and gentle girl who, despite her age, has always been very sheltered from the harsh aspects of life.'

One person who felt the experience would do Shilpa good – and, rather ironically, put her finger on just what it was that was to lead to such a contretemps was her younger sister Shamita. 'Shilpa is used to living like a princess,' she later said. 'This experience will prove to be just the strengthening tonic she needed to shake her out of her domestic cocoon.'

Others in the industry looked on in frank disbelief (initially, that is). 'If I was Shilpa, I would shoot my agent for getting me into this without finding out enough about the programme,' said one.

But clearly Shilpa felt she could do with the exposure. She was also getting well rewarded, but, given that she was paid more than her *Big Brother* fee for every film she made, and she'd made 51 before entering the house, she didn't need the money, either. A whole new career in the West seemed to be what was at stake.

And it was a risk. It later emerged that Shilpa was not the first Bollywood star to be approached by Endemol: at least two other major names were said to have turned down an invitation to appear on the show because they were worried about the impact it would have on their careers. There was also a certain amount of debate about how famous Shilpa really was. Initially presented as being top of the A-list, that turned out to be a bit of an exaggeration: many Bollywood insiders believed that, although she was only 31, her career might have been past its best and this was a last-ditch attempt to get noticed in the West.

'She is known for her body and her face, not her acting,' said Rekha Ahuja, a film producer who worked in Bollywood for a decade and a half. 'She is more of a Penelope Cruz than a Nicole Kidman, but she's a sex symbol for young men, who plaster her posters all over their walls. There is no doubt that she still sells cinema tickets but at her age I imagine that's why she wants to try to sell herself to the American or European film market. I don't think she's good enough, but I admire her for trying.'

Another person who felt that Shilpa was using the show to give her career a new lease of life was Anil Dharker, a socialite based in Bombay and someone with first-hand experience of show business – his daughter Ayesha played the lead role in the London musical *Bombay Dreams*. 'She is not an A-plus star, she is more in the A-minus,' he said. 'But, in a country with several hundred movie stars, only a handful are considered to be true superstars. She is not among the elite.'

Others were a lot more complimentary. 'Everyone, from these people in the urban centres to those in the smallest villages, will see the latest Bollywood film, which offers an escape from normal life,' said Mihir Bose, author of *Bollywood: A History*. 'Actors like Shilpa Shetty cannot walk down the street without being mobbed by fans.'

The singer and dancer Honey Kalaria, now based in Britain, also tried to explain what life for Shilpa was really like. 'Bollywood films give the viewer all the excitement, music, lavish sets and high drama audiences used to expect from Hollywood legends like Gene Kelly,' she said. 'Indian audiences, they won't have it any other way!' As for the actors: 'Once you have a fan base, suddenly you have these audiences that are fans for life. We have quite close-knit communities and family groups, so you'll find that, if one person says, "they're great", everyone else thinks so. It's very rare that people will put a star down.

There are lots of affairs going on and hot and spicy gossip but it's funny how people really thrive on that. They just love it. In their own environment, they are the stars. They are the kings and the queens and they have millions of followers.'

In the event, of course, Shilpa's gamble was to pay off spectacularly well. For a start, her age was no obstacle. Hollywood and its various European counterparts might be obsessed with age but at 31 Shilpa was still younger than Sharon Stone had been when she made her name in *Basic Instinct* (the type of role, incidentally, it is almost inconceivable Shilpa would ever take on). As for acting ability – well, what really is ability? As interest grew, in the West clips began to be shown of Shilpa doing what she does best – dancing – and looking quite spectacularly striking while she was about it. Perhaps she might not be the greatest actress ever to appear on the silver screen, but her appearance, talents and massively heightened profile meant that ultimately she played a very clever game.

There were 10 other inmates – 'celebrities' seems too far-fetched a word to use of all of them. They were Jermaine Jackson (elder brother of Michael), Ken Russell, the 79-year-old veteran filmmaker who had been a highly controversial figure in his youth, a couple of singers (Leo Sayer and Jo O'Meara), another rocker, Donny Tourette, Dirk Benedict, who made his name in *The A-Team*, musician Ian H Watkins, actress Cleo Rocos, columnist Carole Malone and Danielle Lloyd, a model recently stripped of her Miss Great Britain title. Right from the start, Shilpa cut an entirely different figure. Commenting that she would miss her entourage, the best body in Bollywood didn't look overly thrilled when she saw the size of her bed (she was lucky to get one – there were 10 for 11 people), before being advised by Dirk to 'let go'.

Some of the entrances into the house were dramatic, others less so. Donny Tourette of punk band The Towers of London merrily traded insults with the crowd outside while Danielle Lloyd, who had lost her title because she started a relationship with one of the judges, Teddy Sheringham, was booed. Ken Russell proclaimed himself a '*Big Brother* fan', while Jo O'Meara, who had been in S Club 7 and was now a dog breeder, admitted to Davina, 'I am absolutely terrified, I can't tell you how scared I am.'

Not so Leo Sayer who announced as he went in it was 'something to do in January in the rain'. Dirk Benedict took the whole thing a little more in his stride. He turned up in a large van, the replica of the one that had appeared in *The A-Team*, smoking a huge cigar. Fans waiting outside were ecstatic and huge cheers greeted him as he made his way into the house.

The early days were fairly uneventful. Shilpa kept nearly falling off her narrow bed, while an attempt at a meditation session with Ken ended when he suffered a coughing fit. Ironically, given the meal that was to be made of her own name, everyone, including the man himself, was amused at Shilpa's inability to say 'Dirk' properly. Dirk, who appeared rather smitten, claimed he preferred her pronunciation to the correct one. The only other early controversy surrounded snoring, with each housemate accusing all the others of the crime, with Shilpa herself, very much to her surprise, dragged in. This is not how they behaved to stars in India, it seemed – but for now, all was pretty much calm.

It was not until a couple of days later that the real make-up of the house was revealed, and that came on day four. It had been an eventful day: for a start, Donny walked out. However, what really put the cat among the pigeons was the arrival of three brand-new and unexpected housemates: Jade Goody, who had become famous through her participation in the non-celebrity version of *Big Brother* in 2002, her boyfriend Jack Tweedy and her mother Jackiey Budden. Right from the start there were indications of rows to come. Jackiey addressed Shilpa as 'Shil', while Jade and Jack opted for 'Shuppie'.

Viewers, however, were ecstatic at the entrance of the newcomers. Wildly popular among certain segments of the nation's youth, Jade had become something of a role model for anyone wanting to take part in reality TV. Born and brought up in Bermondsey to a lesbian mother and a heroin addict father, who had died a couple of years previously, she was unquestionably *Big Brother*'s greatest success to date. And, indeed, it seemed as if there was something admirable about her. A former dental nurse, she laughed off the quite foul abuse she herself had been subjected to on her first time in the show. Shamefully, she left the house to viewers holding up posters saying, 'Kill the pig' and promptly put the money she had earned into being taught how to read and write. An unlikely career in the media followed, in which she went on to accumulate a multimillion-pound fortune, making herself a heroine along the way to everyone who had been born into a rotten background with seemingly no other way out. *Big Brother* had been the making of Jade: no one, least of all the lady herself, could have dreamed it would also prove her undoing.

Jade seemed supremely confident upon her entrance. 'We're the Goody family,' she announced, before realising that none of the three housemates present had the faintest idea who any of them were – Shilpa and Jermaine were, after all, not English and Ken Russell didn't look like a devotee of reality TV. 'I'm Jade,' she continued. 'I was voted the 25th most infilential [sic] person in the world.' With that, she removed herself to the Diary Room to recount how it felt to be back on the set of *Big Brother*.

There were hints right from the start that the new arrivals might not go down too well with the group already in situ. 'The groups sized each other up – both unhappy at what they saw,' Ken Russell wrote, in a very amusing memoir about the show. 'The intruders saw a plump old codger with white hair, a handsome American and a slim maiden from the East. They smiled – we relaxed. Terrorists don't smile, I thought (erroneously).'

Nor was the scenario Jade and co had walked into designed to relax the inhabitants and soothe any frazzled nerves. Endemol instigated a game called 'Masters and Servants'. The masters – Shilpa, Ken and Jermaine, along with the newcomers – were to remain in the main house, while the servants – everyone else –

were forced to move elsewhere. Servants were expected to wait on masters hand and foot; the masters, meanwhile, were all put up for eviction.

Shilpa had certainly been making her mark. Gaining herself the reputation of being a bit of a diva, she had already asked to change beds because, as a Hindu, she wasn't supposed to sleep with her feet pointing south. She had also been spending some time in the kitchen – an activity that was to become the focal point of the furore – while chatting to Carole about washing up and Jermaine about dried fruits. When the two sets of people were separated, Shilpa gave way to a crying fit – distressed, it seemed, at losing some of her new friends.

It can only be imagined what she thought of the behaviour of the new ones. A four-poster bed was installed in the dormitory for the use of Jade and Jack, who, it appeared, were more than happy to make use of its inviting sheets. Shilpa was famously chaste, having only ever had one serious boyfriend (or perhaps two, if rumours were to be believed). Indeed, this was to become one of the many factors that set Shilpa and Jade apart in the show: the natural delicacy and fastidiousness of the former against the earthiness of the latter. In retrospect, it was bound to end in tears.

It didn't take long at all for the real problems to begin. Jackiey either wouldn't, or couldn't, pronounce Shilpa's name properly, giving rise to the first proper spat between the two of them in the loo. Shilpa, who by now had a cold, was chastened afterwards – 'I never argue and here I am coming to England having a row,' she said. 'I should have kept my calm.' She did, however, go on to reveal that her little sister Shamita had told her not to 'take any shit from anyone'.

At that stage, however, it didn't seem to go any further than that. Dirk still appeared to have a serious crush on the actress, actually blushing when he was teased about it. Ken, meanwhile, was responsible for the next real shock. Following in Donny's footsteps, he walked off the show, complaining that he simply could not deal with the vulgarity and mouthiness of Jade and her family. This caused quite a stir and, given that Ken, possibly more able to look after himself than anyone else in the household, simply couldn't bear the proximity with Jade and her crowd, it speaks volumes for Shilpa that she actually managed to stay the course. She went on to have far more to complain about than he ever did and bore it with extraordinarily good grace.

What finally prompted his departure was a row about food: he helped himself to some crackers, an action to which Jade took offence – technically one of the servants should have served him his food. Soon afterwards, he walked out, calling himself 'fuddy duddy' and saying that some of the surprises were 'a little too much to take'. No one was under any illusion as to which 'surprises' he was talking about; afterwards, he described Jade's onslaught as 'a non-stop stream of top-of-the-lungs abuse that was both unwarranted and obscene'. Ken might have been one of the major controversialists of the day in his time, but he couldn't take such ill-educated vulgarity, and it was left to Carole to tell the others he'd left the set. 'He was a lovely old man,' she said. 'I shall miss him.'

Jade then accidentally broke Shilpa's glasses. Ominously, it was revealed that her grandparents were to visit the show. The introduction of Jade who – oh, the irony of it – only became a celebrity herself by appearing on the programme, along with her loud and noisome family, was always going to be interesting, to say the least. Clearly, it never occurred to anyone that this ploy might be so successful as to make headlines all over the world. Even a generation ago, the idea of someone like Jade finding a national platform, let alone becoming the centre of attention to politicians and public alike, would have been quite laughable.

But we live in a different society now; one created in part by the makers of *Big Brother*, that exercise in voyeurism masking itself as a social experiment, which has done so much to make crude behaviour mainstream. The Goody clan's antipathy to Shilpa contained the seeds of something really nasty, and perhaps because of this the ratings were shortly to go through the roof.

It was still not obvious what was beginning to happen, however. Indeed, the real interest regarding Shilpa continued to be Dirk's obvious attraction to her, even though, at 61, he was 30 years her senior. Dirk was aware of this, too: 'Even my belt is older than her,' he sadly told Leo.

But it was clearly on his mind. Asked by Danielle if there could be a happy ending, he remarked, 'There already is. Naaaah, I've been flirting with her, I tease her; it makes her happy. Isn't that good? For me it's nothing. When a man meets a woman, it's always the woman that decides. There may be dinner, but it doesn't matter what he does. He can do whatever he can to convince her he is a good guy to be with – even today when the girl does all the stuff.'

It was clearly going to be no dice, though. Shilpa had already told the others – who were only too keen to pass it on to Dirk – that she was only interested in marrying a fellow Indian, to say nothing of the fact that she wasn't interested in an older man.

Perhaps it was the fact that a bona fide Hollywood star was interested in her, albeit one a little past his heyday, or maybe because she appeared to be getting on equally well with Jermaine that around this time there were the first indications that some ugly jealousy was beginning to stir. Danielle's suggestion that Shilpa and Dirk get married live on air in *Big Brother* was greeted with hysterics by Shilpa, after which the other women present began to take an altogether bitchier look at the most glamorous woman in their midst. There was some speculation as to what Shilpa earned from her films, as well as the true nature of her star status. Shilpa had apparently compared herself to Angelina Jolie – not, perhaps, the best way of endearing herself to her fellow housemates – a claim the others were only too happy to dispute. Even so, there was still no hint as to quite how nasty matters were to become.

The following day, the atmosphere began to worsen. A mini-row broke out between Jackiey and Shilpa, over ordering a bottle of lemon juice from the food store. Shilpa, said Jackiey, was too controlling. At this point,

Jade and Danielle joined in, deciding Shilpa was too bossy. Shilpa looked utterly bewildered by the venom but contented herself with saying that, in India, this conversation would not have taken place. With commendable self-control, she managed not to retaliate, saying she would not shame her parents by indulging in such abuse herself.

Some days later, after Jackiey's departure, Shilpa's mother Sunanda commented on how well her daughter had behaved. 'Her [Jade's] mother and I could not be farther apart,' she said. 'I found her to be very obnoxious. And when Jackiey was rude to Shilpa, she maintained her dignity because, over here, you don't mistreat your elders.'

Ouch! Could anything have been calculated to dig deeper at the hapless Jackiey? Not only had she been rude and insulting to a visitor to her country but one who was a lot younger than her too.

By this point, the only other woman present who seemed to be sticking up for Shilpa was Carole, advising her to stay out of Jackiey's way. This might have been the first moment at which Shilpa herself began to have qualms about what was going on: 'I don't know what I am doing here,' she admitted. 'It is not really my scene ... I do like most of the people here.'

Alas, it was not a sentiment reciprocated in all quarters. Though the men still seemed pretty enamoured of her, the women were beginning to show a very unpleasant tendency to gang up.

3

About the House

Jackiey, initially, was the worst offender. Despite the fact that it was hardly a difficult one to master, she refused point blank to pronounce Shilpa's name properly, referring to her as 'the Indian'. She continuously made barbed remarks to Shilpa, which may or may not have been the reason why she was the first housemate to be evicted. Shilpa was 'jarring me big time', she informed the world when she did her exit interview, but she was not, unfortunately, alone in her feelings. The bullying – for that is what it had become – only intensified with her absence. Stuck in the *Big Brother* household, Shilpa may have been having an increasingly unpleasant time of it, but her plight was (shamefully) making for gripping TV.

It wasn't all bad. Speculation about Dirk's feelings for Shilpa continued, with Shilpa confessing to Cleo that she found Dirk sexy – but too old. She and Jo also chatted about affairs of the heart, agreeing it is impossible to help who you fall in love with. She also admitted to being interested in the idea of working abroad (almost certainly the reason why she went on *Big Brother* in the first place) before, again, hints of quite unpleasant tensions lurking in the background reappeared. Jade had been making a series of catty remarks about how many servants Shilpa had when she was at home and, clearly increasingly irritated by her attitude, Shilpa asked Dirk if he had ever seen her actually helping to clean up.

The next sign of the rows to come came with the eviction of Carole Malone, possibly Shilpa's biggest remaining ally in the house. Shilpa actually attempted to console Danielle, who responded badly, much to the chagrin of her supporters outside.

'I think things escalated when Carole was evicted. Danielle was so upset because she felt that Shilpa was responsible for Carole leaving the house and that night Danielle had a bit too much to drink and exchanged a few cross words with Shilpa – which she later apologised for,' said Leeandra Anderson, a great friend of Danielle's. 'Danielle will be deeply disheartened when she leaves the house to find out what has gone on in the outside world. I'm sure she will be hurt, but she has the support of her family and friends. We know she's certainly not racist.'

What actually happened was this: Carole, Cleo and Shilpa had been caught discussing nominations, something in direct contravention to the show's rules. However, of the three, only Carole was up for eviction, against Leo and Dirk. In the event, of course, it was Carole who left. She herself, however, was miffed that of the three offenders only she was on the nominations list, and made her feelings very clear to poor Shilpa, and to the others, as well. Indeed, Carole and Danielle teamed up for a little bitch fest of their own, with Danielle moaning, 'Why do you have to go? She's vile!'

'Someone they want to keep in, they don't even involve them,' sniffed Carole.

Unbeknownst to the housemates, of course, concern was rapidly growing on the outside with complaints beginning to flood in, while high-profile Asians living in Britain were appalled at what was going on. 'I think it's disgusting, and I do think that the behaviour shown towards Shilpa is racist,' said the British-based writer, director and actor Manish Patel. 'However, the people involved don't actually realise what they're doing. I think that the reason why Asians in Britain have taken this matter to task is because we actually thought that this problem had disappeared and didn't exist any more. But it's become quite clear that some people do have strong viewpoints about Asians and it is often something that they keep hidden inside. They may say one thing to your face, but behind your back they'll be saying something completely different.'

Indeed, it was not just British Asians but people across the world who were beginning to wonder what modern-day Britain was really like. 'Asian people may well now be wondering just what their white counterparts are really thinking about them,' Manish Patel went on. 'Do people really believe that someone from India eats with their hands? It's quite ridiculous! Shilpa is a guest in our country. The housemates knew that she was different, they were aware that she knew very little about Great Britain and *Big Brother* and, instead of welcoming her, taking the time to find out about her, they have treated her abysmally.'

Back in the house, the men at least remained ardent fans. Dirk overcame his discomfiture at being nominated to leave by flirting even more heavily with Shilpa, while the lady herself continued to confide in

Jermaine. Indeed, her sister was right: the experience did seem to be doing her some good in that she herself said that this was the first time in her life she had ever done anything, including going out on a date, without asking her parents first. (When she went out at night, she always had to be back by 2am.) She seemed to enjoy confiding in Jermaine: 'I'm more chilled out when I'm off camera,' she said. 'I can't do that now because I'll let down all the Indian people who want me to project my culture ... Krishna says you do your karma, do what you have to do, don't wait for the fruits it will bear. People here don't belong to my culture. They don't understand my culture. I don't expect anything but politeness and love.'

Some hope! But she was to get a good deal else out of it instead.

Day 10 in the *Big Brother* house and, although the full extent of what was to come was still not apparent, matters were hotting up. Two contestants had already walked out and now a third joined their ranks: Leo Sayer left after a hissy fit when Big Brother refused to send him more underpants. His abrupt departure might also have had something to do with the fact that he was the favourite to be evicted, but tensions had been building for days now, with the diminutive singer apparently unhappy about being forced to play the role of a servant. At any rate, he was gone now, having made a dramatic escape by bashing down a door with a shovel!

He did, however, have a chat with Davina about why he left. 'It was the underpants ... I'd run out and didn't want to wash my smalls in front of everybody else,' he explained. 'When I got out of the house and looked properly, there was one more [clean] pair! I could have stayed another day. It's a little bit disappointing,' he continued. 'I was tired, my energy went, I wasn't feeling very good. I did lose it a few times ... when you get tired, you get ratty and do silly things.' He hadn't been thrilled about the conditions in which he lived either. 'Sharing the shower and [the house] being really messy,' he said, of the factors that had irritated him. 'I haven't shared a house with people for a long time ... I was ill-prepared mentally.'

Indeed, it was a welcome comic relief from the increasingly nasty atmosphere in the house. The first row about food blew up on the day Leo left, and so to have a distraction was a good morale boost all round. Leo himself was philosophical: asked what he felt about his escape becoming a moment of high comedy, he replied, 'It kind of wasn't very funny for me, but the amazing thing is that it has actually spread all over the globe. I've had people from Australia, San Francisco, people from Los Angeles, friends from New York, friends from Canada, friends from Italy, saying, "Oh my God, we have just downloaded you!" So I am everywhere – if only my records could make such an international impact.'

Like Ken before him, he felt the atmosphere in the house changed the moment the three new arrivals appeared. 'I was trying to be a peacemaker and say we are all going to have to pull together, if you all show each other a bit of love then we can forgive each other afterwards for whatever,' he said. 'But that actually stopped the moment the Goodys came in.'

Funnily enough, he took a considerably more benign view towards them than some of the others did. Asked his opinion of Jackiey, he replied, 'I loved her. She was the saddest exit from the house for me. I think she's great because she's like a child, she's innocent, and if you don't like it you tell her to shut up and she shuts up.'

He was of the opinion that no one else would head for the hills, which was good news for Shilpa, who had been worrying that her friend Jermaine might also want to get out. Instead, she applied cream to her face and began to prepare some food. Not that it was obvious that anything was amiss at the start: all she had to contend with initially was a lovestruck Dirk hanging around her; 'I like your eyes, your laughter – everything,' he said.

'I need help here,' Shilpa called to Jermaine, laughing.

'Jermaine, stay away,' commanded Dirk.

In the background the girls seethed.

As has already been chronicled here, matters then turned extremely nasty, with the row leading Jade declare, 'She makes me feel sick. She makes my skin crawl.'

'She's a dog!' responded Danielle.

Danielle was clearly the worse for wear, but Jermaine felt some responsibility for the unpleasantness, confiding to Big Brother that he shouldn't have got Shilpa to talk to Danielle when the latter was drunk. 'Shilpa is too wise to come between a friendship,' he said. 'I think Danielle's youthfulness provoked all this unintentionally. Shilpa is balanced. She knows how to handle ups and downs. I'm not here to change anyone's life. I'm not going out of my way. That's what Shilpa did, and it got her into trouble.'

Shilpa and Jermaine continued to bond, the latter

saying he thought he'd be leaving soon, while the former attempted to console him and told him there are lessons to be learned from every experience – and, goodness knows, she herself could have testified to that. Jade and Jack had both voted her the person they wanted to be evicted; Shilpa, meanwhile, nominated Jack for doing no work in the house, and Leo, who later left anyway, for verbal diarrhoea. Dirk contented himself with telling Shilpa he needed an Indian woman in his life.

Come the next morning, as complaints continued to flood into Channel 4, the housemates, totally unaware of the growing controversy outside, were given their next task. They were to divide into two groups, who would be called 'Steps' and 'The Jackson Five', in homage, of course, to Ian and Jermaine. Fittingly, Jermaine was the leader of the Jackson Five, with Shilpa, Dirk, Cleo and Danielle also joining the group to sing 'I Want You Back'. The others, as Steps, were to sing 'Deeper Shade of Blue'. Although Shilpa had never heard of the songs involved, this gave her the opportunity to do what she did best: dance. She was also highly complimentary of Jermaine as an instructor, saying that in his place she would have killed everyone, and she told Jermaine and Dirk that Danielle's diatribe the previous evening was down to alcohol and she wasn't taking it personally. This sweetness and forgiveness did nothing to endear her to the other women on the show.

Nor did the fact that, although she didn't exactly distinguish herself in the singing stakes, she made a pretty good fist of dancing in The Jackson Five. The group was dressed up in giant Afro wigs and outfits from the 1970s and pulled it off pretty well, despite Shilpa gasping teasingly, 'We sucked! That was terrible. That's the end of my career.'

Far from it: The Jackson Five won over Steps with 75 per cent of the viewers' vote, while Shilpa, who had clearly enjoyed herself, remarked that this was the best task so far. The winners were awarded a gold disc, along with champagne and chocolate, although Shilpa's confession that she had never heard the song she sang before was utterly mystifying to the rest of the housemates. But then again, why should she have? The fact that she came from a different culture was by now glaringly obvious and the fact that The Jackson Five were not famous in India was surely another indication of their differing backgrounds. It didn't matter – it was one of the rare things that didn't matter by this stage – but it was a graphic illustration of the fact that the housemates, to put it mildly, did not all come from the same place.

And the sniping was getting worse. Shilpa and Cleo had a late-night chat about why Shilpa didn't like Paris. Shilpa declined to enlarge on whether she had ever been there with the wrong person, which was a relief to some viewers as at least it meant that she was speaking to one of the women in the house. The other three, who by now had turned into a thoroughly unpleasant little gang, seemed to be as happy to bitch about Shilpa behind her back as they were to cause unpleasantness to her face. Indeed, so unpleasant was it all becoming that there was open speculation on the outside that Jade might be turfed out (or, at least, that she should be). Still, none of the gang of three had any idea of the impression they were creating – it was left to the friends, family and business advisers outside to realise just how much it was all going horribly wrong.

Inside, Shilpa was practically leading two lives: as a housemate who was lively and got on with all the men, and a housemate horribly victimised by the women. Away from Jade and co, matters were fine, with Shilpa confiding to Jermaine that she'd like to tie the knot.

'I wanna get married,' she said. 'I have done for a long time.'

'Dirk would marry you tomorrow,' said Jermaine. 'He's a nice guy.'

'He's a very, very nice guy,' said Shilpa tactfully. 'I want to get married ... but to the right person. Not just because ...'

'He's about to walk through the door,' said Jermaine of Dirk.

Intriguingly for Shilpa watchers, she allowed herself to be drawn out on the subject of the men in her life. As a sex symbol in India, she had the rather intriguing task of presenting herself as infinitely desirable and yet also infinitely chaste (something else that set her aside from the British contingent), to date having never so much as kissed a man on screen. There have been various rumours about her private life, but very little of actual substance to go on. Shilpa is plainly aware of something else, too: that mystery adds to a person's attractiveness and it is better not to tell all.

At any rate, talking with Jermaine, she was a little more open about her past than she had been to date. There had been one actor, she confided, who had wanted to marry her, but she hadn't felt the same and so they split up. A few months later, he was engaged to someone else. Then there was a long-distance relationship with a musician, which ended because she was more successful than him.

It was then that the notorious chicken row finally blew up. The ugliness that it entailed has already been chronicled here, and the outside world was not alone in expressing concern – some of the other housemates clearly sensed that the gang of three was going much too far. Ian and Cleo both felt the need to talk to Shilpa about it, with Ian saying he thought she was being unnecessarily picked on.

Shilpa rose above it. 'But I tried not to let it affect me,' she said. 'I don't have anything against any of them.'

'You haven't done anything wrong, Shilpa,' said Ian earnestly.

'Maybe we eat food differently,' she replied. 'It's just a culture clash.'

You would have thought that if the girls had had an ounce of self-awareness they might have brought a halt to the nastiness now, but that appeared not to be the case. Instead, matters rumbled on in the background, while Shilpa herself simply tried to get on with it. For a start, she expressed a desire to go to Yorkshire – and then worried that no one in Yorkshire would know who she was.

'Of course,' protested Ian. '*Big Brother*'s the biggest show on television.' He was certainly right about how much her fame had already spread.

The flirtation with Dirk continued, although perhaps because some of the other men had by now jumped ship, he was in an unusually tetchy mood. 'I'm sure girls' dormitories are like this,' he said. 'This is such a girlie show – that's why all the guys left. It drives you nuts!'

'I've not driven you nuts,' said Shilpa, sounding rather hurt.

'No,' responded Dirk hastily. He, too, was in a mood for confessions: it had been 15 years, he said, since he'd been properly involved in a relationship and even two years since he'd last had a date. Shilpa looked sympathetic and friendly but, again, didn't take him up on it.

Another entertainment was introduced in the form of a ping-pong table. Alone among the girls, Shilpa played with Dirk, Ian and Jermaine. But the stress of being cooped up with one another for nearly two weeks was now plainly beginning to tell: a few people were looking fed up and tetchy. Circumstances were trying, to say the least, with everyone affected by the bad atmosphere in the house and not just Shilpa. Dirk was right; the feeling was of a particularly bitchy girls' boarding school and everyone was beginning to feel a touch of ennui.

'I miss my friends,' said Ian. 'I'm used to being away, that's part of my job, but I'm not used to not having any contact. I miss my dog.'

'I probably need to have my mobile surgically removed,' confessed Shilpa.

'It's probably good that you're not using it because of the radiation,' Jermaine remarked.

Showing a quite extraordinary tolerance, given all that had gone before, Shilpa now started to try to explain the concept of the Hindu festival of Diwali to Jade. It was a valiant attempt, but one that didn't stand a chance. Shilpa had just got to Rama, when Jade enquired, 'Is that the Elephant Man?'

Shilpa, rather more politely than Jade deserved, informed her that she was thinking of Ganesha.

Even Big Brother, however, could not have foreseen the next bit of multicultural misunderstanding. The housemates were instructed to come up with a question they have always wanted to know the answer to, and Shilpa thought of a good one – which came first, the chicken or the egg? That was probably too clever for some of the others, though, and so Jo came up with an alternative. The following exchange ensued:

Jo: I've got my question – what is the life span of a sperm whale?

Shilpa: What's the lifespan of a what?

Jo: Of a sperm whale.

Shilpa: Of a spom …?

Jo: A whale. A sperm whale is a type of whale.

Shilpa: A wow? What's that?

Jo: Am I saying it wrong?

Jade (to Shilpa): Beached whale, killer whale … like a dolphin.

Jack: Have you seen *Free Willy*?

Jo: You really don't know what a whale is?

Jack: In the sea …

Jade: You know what a shark is, don't you?

Shilpa finally got it, knowing exactly what a whale was – she simply hadn't understood Jo's cockney accent. It did provoke a laugh. But by this time everyone was so sour almost anything could have done it, and later on Jade turned nasty again, although, at the beginning at least, she and Shilpa appeared to be trying to make up. Jade's comments about Shilpa's cooking were not personal, she said, adding that she couldn't work out if Shilpa was genuinely upset. She then suggested she stop cooking. This seemed to upset poor Shilpa all over again: she rushed sobbing to the loos, where Cleo was on hand to comfort her. It was hardly surprising it was getting to her – earlier in the day, Danielle had remarked, 'I'm fucking pissed off! I want to rip someone's head off. She's an annoying bitch.' Outside, her advisers groaned.

Outside, of course, there was by now an absolute furore, but still the housemates themselves were totally unaware of what was going on. Shilpa, wearing a large pair of sunglasses to hide swollen eyes, emerged in the morning to be comforted by Jermaine and Cleo, both of whom appeared horrified by what was going on. Neither, however, for whatever reason, was able to stop it, and told Shilpa, probably rightly, that it all boiled down to a clash of cultures. Still trying hard to be reasonable to everyone, Shilpa said that she appreciated Jade's honesty. Elsewhere in the house, not only was this graciousness not reciprocated but matters swiftly went from bad to worse.

Jade decided to tell the others about a nightmare she'd just had: that Shilpa was kicking her and Shilpa's cousin appeared to pull Danielle's hair. Whether this was her conscience telling her that this was pretty much what she deserved, or merely an attempt to gang up on Shilpa even more, it actually seemed to provoke a small crisis in Danielle. Despite the fact that she had been joining in the unpleasantness with gusto, she went to the bedroom to tell Shilpa that no one had bad feelings towards her and that she didn't want her to be left out. This unlikely rapprochement was not to last. For a moment, at least, hostilities were suspended, with Shilpa even offering her some cream to soothe her skin. Danielle accepted, but was soon back on the rampage once more.

Amidst all of this, Shilpa was conscious that not only did she have to put on a good show for herself when it came to being in the house, but that she was, after all, representing India as well. And so, when Jermaine expressed an interest in the Taj Mahal, Shilpa was able to tell him that the emperor Shahjehan built it for his wife Mumtaz and then cut off the hands of the builders so that they could not build another one like it. Jermaine looked suitably impressed by this gory tale.

Ian, it appeared, was interested in India, too: namely, was it acceptable for women to show a bit of cleavage? No problem, said Shilpa – as long as it was tastefully done.

The next test was set. The housemates were to dress up in splendid clothing for a red-carpet event, which turned out to be a red-carpet assault course in which they had an obstacle race through a VIP pit filled with rubbish, a Champagne Fountain and a Crawl of Fame. If they got through it in nine minutes, they would receive luxury provisions; if they failed, it would just be the basics. Hampered by formal evening clothes, it actually took 10 minutes for the housemates to crawl through. This meant that only basic rations were available, which went on to provoke yet another row, when Jo accused Shilpa of being too controlling. This time Shilpa refused to be upset and told Cleo how funny it was that people ended up fighting over tea and ketchup. It was a very good point.

Dirk's pursuit, meanwhile, was as ardent as ever. On hearing that Shilpa had been born in 1975, he commented that he was reborn in 1975. He also said that he wanted to see Shilpa in a film in which she was the seductress.

'You should see *Dus* – it means 10,' Shilpa told him.

'You did 10?' asked a slightly gobsmacked Dirk.

'I was an ATC agent – a very serious kind of movie, the first time ever a heroine did an action sequence,' she replied. 'I jump and I kick.'

'When did you do that?' asked Dirk.

'Two years back,' Shilpa replied.

But, elsewhere in the house, the unpleasantness

continued. Jade and Jo continued to bitch about Shilpa, now deciding that it was her laugh that was an irritant. Jade imitated her saying, 'Eeeeek!' Jo said she had to go out of the room when Shilpa laughed. By this time, with the clamour outside reaching ever new heights, Channel 4 bosses were beginning to realise that they must somehow bring all this bullying and savagery to an end.

4
Two Weeks In

It seems amazing, in retrospect, that the housemates could have had so little idea about the upset they had created in the outside world, but that, of course, is the nature of *Big Brother*. The band of three continued to dig themselves an ever deeper hole blithely unaware of what they were doing, while the various stresses and strains of the group waxed and waned. At times, it was almost possible to believe that Jade actually did have some interest in Shilpa's culture; at others, it merely seemed as if she was trying to bait her in any way possible. By the end of the second week, a discussion on teenage pregnancies ensued, with Jade showing a mixture of aggression and genuine curiosity as she quizzed Shilpa about her own attitudes. Was Shilpa progressive? she asked.

'Of course I am,' she replied, pointing out the fact that she was 31. 'We were brought up with the belief that you should get married so when I had my first boyfriend we were very close and I thought this was the be-all and end-all for me. I think I'm someone who's not against premarital sex but I'm totally against someone who just has sex. I couldn't get into a physical relationship with someone if I wasn't emotionally attached.'

Of course, Jade was totally unaware that she had touched on an area of enormous interest to Shilpa's fans. While she had been known to have boyfriends, it was unclear quite how close the relationships had become, and Shilpa, who was well aware of the power of discretion, wasn't about to let on. She didn't even like saying the 's' word.

'You can use the word, it isn't dirty,' said Ian, who had been listening in with a good deal of interest.

'I don't usually say that word – I'm silly and say "making love",' said Shilpa coyly.

'Having sex and making love is completely different,' Jade chimed in.

As ever, it wasn't long before matters got completely

out of hand, and yet again this involved food. For some reason, the kitchen seemed to bring out the worst in the women, the offending ingredients this time round being a few chicken stock cubes. Rather than managing to discuss things reasonably, Jade, as ever, flew off the handle. 'So what, it's a stock cube, get over it!' she yelled. 'The other day a whole chicken went to waste because it was pink. Not only are you pathetic and fake, you're a liar!'

Up until now, Shilpa had been taking it all remarkably well, given the amount of aggravation she had had to endure, but it was quite clear she had had enough. Even gracious Bollywood actresses who like to stay reserved have their breaking points and she appeared to be getting remarkably close to hers. For the first time, she pointed out what was patently obviously true – that the other women didn't like her because she got on so well with Ian, Dirk and Jermaine – while Ian himself, clearly on her side, told her to forget about the chicken episode. Matters, more than ever, were coming to a head.

But so unaware was Jade of the impression she had created that she retired to the Diary Room with a list of complaints about Shilpa. Among a good deal else, she moaned, Shilpa was getting on Jack's nerves (poor

Jack!), she was controlling, she had an agenda, her screeching was irritating and, every time Jade spoke to her, Shilpa would cry.

And so it went on, but, much as the aggravation from the girls continued, the flirting went on with the boys. Dirk's ardour wasn't dented by the malevolence in the background and, when Shilpa was hanging up clothes and picked up a broken hanger, he was immediately by her side to help. The following exchange took place:

Shilpa: No, please. I know you're really strong and all of that.

Dirk: Come here, I am really good at fixing things.

Shilpa: Thank you! Are you gonna keep the hanger as well, to remember me by?

Ian (in the background): Will she, won't she?

Dirk: Ian, I don't need any help from you.

Ian: You flirt as much as you want. Get a room, you two, get a room!

Perhaps it was the fact that the men were so obviously keen that made the girls even madder, for that night, as Shilpa slept, unaware of what they were saying about her, an even uglier exchange took place. 'I think it's nasty and she's very, very manipulative,' said Jade. 'Very. In my eyes she's a nasty piece of work. I look at her and I wanna headbutt her, I wanna wipe that smug look off her face! Because I'm so not fake and genuinely real, I can see it [Shilpa] not being genuine.'

'You're fucking bang on and I'm the fairest person in the world,' said Jo.

'Shall we go lift her up and put her in the garden, then lock the door?' asked Jack.

What were they thinking of? Or were they thinking at all? Ganging up to pick on one woman is bad enough, but threatening physical violence? Still it went on. It was now that Jade announced that she thought Shilpa could be a fraud – 'For all I know, she could be someone from up Old Kent Road.'

Of course, the sheer nastiness of all of this aside, there was actually a reason why Jade was voicing her doubts, which could be summed up in one word: Chantelle. The previous year, *Big Brother* bosses had put a non-celebrity, Chantelle Houghton, into the house. Chantelle managed to fool the other participants into thinking that she was, in fact, famous, and of course she actually became famous in the course of it all. Jade was clearly wondering if this year the producers had pulled a similar trick.

They hadn't, of course, for, had she but realised it, this year's trick was none other than Jade herself. To have picked a cast of celebrities then utterly disrupted proceedings by putting the Goody clan into the midst of it all certainly livened things up. Even before the rows with Shilpa began, two inmates were sent scurrying out for freedom. Outside now, controversy continued to rage – effigies were being burned, with senior politicians being dragged into it all, while the entire nation of India was outraged. The house, meanwhile, carried on as usual.

Well, almost as usual. There were signs that the male members of the household were becoming increasingly concerned about Shilpa: the gang of three had by now become so nasty, so malevolent and so deeply unpleasant they were clearly wondering if there was anything they could do. 'When Jade was going off at Shilpa the other girls were laughing,' said Jermaine. 'They are being controlled by Jade, it's ignorance. It's become territorial now. I'm trying to be neutral but I'm not going to let things be unfair. I'm not willing to talk to Jade; I can't change Jade.'

'In her mind, she's right,' said Ian.

'She [Jade] told her [Shilpa] that her head was so far up her own arse she could smell her own shit,' said

Jermaine, clearly unable to believe the vulgarity to which the girls had sunk.

Danielle appeared to have been struck by her conscience, though. Of the three girls, she was the most ambivalent towards Shilpa, sometimes radiating hostility and yet at other times she appeared to want to be friends. This is, of course, not an unknown situation where bullying arises: one person leads the way and, through strength of personality, forces the others to follow, whether they want to or not. That is not to excuse Danielle of any culpability, but at times her hostility towards Shilpa showed signs of abating, especially after a particularly unpleasant row. 'Shilpa, I don't like arguing with anyone and I don't want to argue with you,' she said, following the housemate into the bathroom the morning after the latest spat.

'Don't worry, I'm cool,' said Shilpa, giving Danielle a hug. 'You were never like that with me.'

'I don't want you to feel left out, I feel really bad and I'm not a bad person,' said Danielle.

'You are not a bad person,' responded Shilpa reassuringly. 'And neither is Jo … and neither is Jade. Jade just waits for an argument and I'm not like that. I can't be what she wants me to be. I don't have anything against you, trust me.'

It was pretty nice of her, all things considered, but Jade would not be satisfied. She alternated between ignoring Shilpa to her face and bitching viciously about her behind her back. Now there was no common ground to be found, no rapprochement until the very end of Jade's stay when what she had done finally dawned on her.

It must be said that it was also around now that Danielle had announced that Shilpa should 'fuck off home' – yet another remark that provoked outcry on the outside. In the Diary Room, perhaps the very first sign that the producers felt they had better warn the girls of what they were doing, she was asked what she meant by that. Danielle said she had forgotten all about it, regretted being so offensive and was disgusted with herself. It was an early version of what Jade was to say, but the implicit warning seems to have gone unheeded. Everyone carried on much as before.

Still, somehow, the housemates managed to keep going, congratulating themselves on having managed to survive a fortnight in the house, before the conversation got on to the rock band Queen. This is one that Shilpa had heard of: indeed, she pointed out that the late, great Freddie Mercury was himself of Indian origin. The gang of three did not appear to be impressed.

Big Brother was setting the housemates another task: this time they were to divide into groups of three and create a work of modern art illustrating an emotion they had felt during their time in the house. Shilpa's collaborators were to be Ian and Jermaine. Together, the three decided to use the feeling of strength as their inspiration. They made a cardboard torso, with a bent right arm and a red heart painted in the middle. 'This explains the strength we all try to show in every situation, even in times we are really distressed,' said Shilpa, managing to keep a straight face. 'It doesn't just denote physical strength, but also in terms of character.'

Dirk now appeared to be becoming philosophical about the fact that, in reality, he and Shilpa were very unlikely to have a romance. He, too, seemed to think the age difference would create a problem, even going so far as to hint that he might have been putting some of it on. 'Shilpa, it's fun, I can make her giggle and blush,' he said. 'If I was younger, she would interest me. But the truth is, she was very nice about it, she handled it well. She could have not liked it at all, said, "I don't find this appealing, it's not attractive, it's not charming, it's not funny, stop it," which I would have done.'

In fact, the flirting provided a very welcome relief

from the viciousness marring the show. It also meant Shilpa had some allies – even if they were, as she herself pointed out, mostly the men.

But that veiled warning to Danielle about the comments they were making had not been enough. Racism on *Big Brother* was now the major issue of the day; almost every newspaper had it on the front page, while even people who had never seen the show knew about the controversy. With Jade's advisers desperate for her to shut up, the subject was broached directly in the Diary Room: just what had she meant by saying 'Shilpa Fuckawallah' and 'Shilpa Poppadom'?

'Shilpa Poppadom,' said Jade musingly. 'I explained that for the other two trying to get her name out. Her name is not Shilpa Harry or Shilpa Tweed or Shilpa Mackintosh, she is Indian, so will have an Indian name. No racial anything. She is Indian, [I was] thinking of an Indian name and [the] only thing I could think of was Indian food. Wasn't racial at all; it was not to offend any Indian out there. Everyone knows I don't like her; she don't like me. What I said about her was not meant in a racial way – it's not acceptable if done in that way. Mine wasn't done in that way.'

Shilpa herself finally pronounced on the great race debate. 'You know, when I actually thought about it, I know it's not a racist thing,' she said. 'I thought about it for a long time. It's not racist. You know people say things in anger. She [Jade] tries to challenge me. She tries to challenge my beliefs.'

It was a generous attitude. Jaws dropped still further later in the day when Jade and Shilpa actually hugged one another. Remarkably, Jade sounded a lot more contrite than she had in the past.

'I know that what has happened has not been nice for you and a lot of stuff got said the other day from you and from myself,' said Jade, somewhat inarticulately to Shilpa. 'I didn't say [Shilpa Poppadom] in a racial way ... I do not judge people by the colour of their skin.'

'I know that,' said Shilpa, whose graciousness was now such that, whatever the outcome of *Big Brother*, she was a winner all the way. 'I don't think you're racist.'

'I appreciate you saying that,' said Jade. 'It does mean a lot.' (It might actually have meant the rescue of Jade's career as by now the lady herself was perhaps horribly aware.)

'If somebody is going to keep calling me fake, it's bound to hurt me,' said Shilpa, not unreasonably.

In this new spirit of cooperation, it now emerged that what had really upset Jade was Shilpa telling her she needed elocution classes.

'I didn't say "elocution", I said "etiquette",' said Shilpa, unwittingly adding a comic element.

'It's obvious we don't get on,' responded Jade, sounding humble. 'Different backgrounds.'

'There is definitely a culture clash,' said Shilpa. 'You said more nasty things about me than I said about you.'

'I was angry of the fact that I'd let you make me get so angry over a cube!' explained Jade. 'I don't want the awkwardness any more. It's an awkward situation and I don't like it. I'm not spiteful and I'm not purposely nasty. I'm sorry.'

There was going to be an awful lot more of that to come.

The two then hugged, much to the relief of the rest of the house, who had been subjected to the nonsense all along. And then, in the spirit of what might be called *Big Brother perestroika*, Danielle got in on the act.

'I didn't agree with some of the things you said to Jade, but I especially didn't agree with some of the things that Jade said to you,' she said contritely, as they were all getting ready to go to bed. 'I hate confrontation, I hate arguing.'

'[Jade and I] had a very good conversation outside,' said Shilpa magnanimously. 'We cleared it all out. She doesn't need to be worried.'

'I'm sorry,' said Danielle, by now sounding as humble as Jade. ''Cos I'm young and quite naive, I've probably took the route where I'll stick with Jade. I feel really disgusted at myself ... I'm following the leader, following the group when [you are] a really nice girl. I'm not a bad person, I have got a good heart.'

'You have to have your own identity,' said Shilpa wisely.

'Since Jade came, I've felt really intimidated because Jade's a much stronger person,' said Danielle.

What has caused Jade and Danielle to express a change of heart towards Shilpa led to much speculation. We may never know the cause. Perhaps the real question was whether it was to prove too little too late to save their careers. Even so, everyone appeared to be relieved that the atmosphere had calmed down – the sheer emotional level at which they were all pitched had created an almost unbearable tension, even for those who were not involved.

There had been a great deal of activity on the outside, however, and so the next morning Shilpa and Jade were told that one of them would be evicted from the house that night. It was the only surefire way of bringing the row to an end, so, even if they hadn't pushed for it, Channel 4 bosses must have been relieved. And, looking back, the outcome was inevitable, although that was not immediately clear in the house.

'I knew I'd be up,' said Jade glumly.

'Me too,' Shilpa chimed in.

'Whoever goes will be happy, and they can sleep in their own bed,' said Ian tactfully.

'Yeah, and, when I find out who nominated me, I won't speak to them ever again,' said Jade.

Alas, that was to be the least of her worries when she got out, and she was clearly well aware of it. 'Shilpa says she knows I'm not racist, but the press have a lot of power and if they want to print I'm racial [sic] that could influence a lot of people and I could be evicted for the wrong reasons,' she said. 'Fair enough if people vote me out because they don't like me, but if it's because they think I'm a racist bitch I'll be worried about walking out because that's not me.'

By now, all the housemates seemed to sense quite how serious matters had become. Jade herself was fretting constantly, even bringing up an occasion when she had been to India herself. Shilpa remained extremely gracious, continuing to express concern for Jade. She, too, seemed to realise that a lot was at stake here as far as Jade's future was concerned and that urgent crisis management was required. 'I don't want Jade to feel that I've spoiled all that she's made for herself,' she said. 'I really wish that from the bottom of my heart. I have a life back in India and that's going to be unaffected, really.' Little did Shilpa realise at this juncture what an international sensation she had made.

And so, finally, to the eviction. There were no crowds outside and it was strongly suspected that Jade's subsequent interview with Davina was not as live as it looked, for the interview was nothing like as searching as the ones she was about to get. But all that was still to come.

'Why's it so quiet?' asked Danielle.

'I know why it's quiet,' said Jade. 'What I said the other day, I know. I don't know why I came back in here.'

'I just nearly suffered a heart attack,' Shilpa said after the announcement had been made. 'You will be OK,' she continued to Jade. 'There's nothing to fear.'

'Don't start me crying,' said Jade. 'I don't want to cry.'

'I don't want her to go out like this,' Shilpa confided anxiously to Ian. 'I pray to God there's no problem for her out there. If I went out today I would have defended her.'

She returned to Jade: 'It always works out for the best in the long run,' she said.

'I've been in this situation before – I'm the 25th most intellectual person,' Jade responded.

'Influential,' said Shilpa.

And so Jade went.

Things were certainly a lot quieter after that, but, although Jade was gone, she was most certainly not forgotten. The following day, Shilpa and Jermaine discussed the situation, with the latter, at least, delighted at the turn of events. 'It's amazing,' he said. 'The situation and how it evolved and what was said, and how her followers ... it was amazing. Wasn't it? Amazing! It's just good to know that people out there still look for the good in people because I'm pretty sure if I was acting ugly in here, I'd be out of here. It doesn't matter who you are, you just can't be cruel.'

Shilpa, however, was surprised that it was she, rather than Jade, who was left in the house.

'Did you think that you were going to be leaving?' asked Jermaine.

'Yeah,' said Shilpa. 'Because she kept telling me that, you know, she has a huge fan base. She was saying to all of us that she had so many fans and people come up to her all the time telling her how much she's loved and she's the 20th most influential person in the world.'

'That means nothing,' Jermaine replied. 'What took place was about just being right, being right. And if you're so famous and you're wrong, you're wrong. If you're not famous and you're right, you're right.'

'In the Diary Room when they asked me, "How would you feel if you left and do you want to stay?" I said, "I don't know, I accept it either way,"' Shilpa went on. 'I'm prepared to go because I learned that Jade has a great fan base here and I know I have my fan base in all the Indians and Pakistanis and Bangladeshis, and I said, "If they [the public] want me to be in here they'll keep me in here, and if they don't want me in here they'll vote me out so I accept their decision."'

Perhaps it was the relief of having Jade out of her hair, but rather unexpectedly Shilpa chose the occasion to try some of Danielle's cider. 'I think I am a little high,' she said afterwards. 'I am a cheap date.'

If truth be told, Jade's eviction seemed to be playing on a few other minds as well. She was not, after all, the only person to have engaged in bullying and to have screeched abuse, and it clearly began to occur to Jo and Danielle that, if Jade was in trouble because of what had happened, then they might just be, too.

'You OK?' Shilpa asked Jo after they'd all gone to bed for the night.

'It's just I'm really nervous, I can't switch my mind off,' said Jo fretfully. 'Can't you sleep either?'

'I was thinking about how to reinvent you,' Shilpa replied. 'I swear to God, I was thinking of what outfit to give you, you are so good!'

'I'm so worried but I don't know why,' said Jo.

'You're just anxious,' said Shilpa, who by this time was clearly going for nomination as a saint. 'Everything is well outside, just keep saying that. There must be so many people out there who would love to be in your shoes.'

'I don't want to be in my shoes,' said Jo. 'Not at the moment.'

'Shut up!' cried Shilpa. 'This is a good thing for you!'

'I'm panicking about when it's my time to go through the door,' said Jo.

'You have a great body, you have a great attitude, you have a great voice,' said Shilpa. 'If you have it, show it. You have a great ass, show it!'

'You're very sweet,' said Jo.

5

The Countdown Begins

Life after Jade, it must be said, was considerably quieter. With their leader gone, Jo, Danielle and Jack all stopped baiting Shilpa – although there was to be another upset from a surprising quarter before the series was over – and there was even some semblance of harmony among the housemates as they took to their manifold tasks. The latest was to dress up as satin- and lycra-clad showgirls and take part in routines. Though the result was pretty awful, the viewers were kept entertained, and Big Brother deemed it good enough to award them champagne and chocolate as well as luxury items on the next day's shopping list.

Outside, had they but known it, Jade had started on her *mea culpa* tour, while questions continued to be raised about the furore. The fact that Shilpa herself had said that she thought the bullying had not been racist did nothing to calm anyone down, although, given the massive wave of British public support towards Shilpa, at least Britain's reputation as a tolerant country had been restored. Increasingly, Jade's actions were seen as an aberration rather than the norm, while the lady herself was doing everything she could to put matters right.

Speculation was beginning to grow that Shilpa might actually win *Big Brother*. The fact that she had reacted towards all the girls with such good grace was testimony to her own character, while Britain itself seemed to be seeing this as a way of making amends. After all, if Shilpa won the show, Britain could not possibly be called a racist nation, and could be seen as one that was so anti-racism that it gave its support to a person who might have been the victim of it. And the nation's obsession with Shilpa seemed stronger than ever.

Pictures of her in exotic attire appeared in the papers every day that passed; if nothing else, the row had given Fleet Street the opportunity to print ever more glamorous photos of Shilpa. Inside the house, she herself protested that she was usually a jeans and T-shirt kind of a gal; outside, her appearance grew ever more sultry with every new still that appeared. Quite a substantial part of the nation seemed to be in love with Shilpa or, at least, absolutely fascinated by her. She was a bird of paradise nestling, for a short time, on a grey little island absolutely delighted by the warmth and colour she brought with her.

Meanwhile, in India further details came to light as to how she ended up on the show. The original choice had been Lara Dutta; others included the actress Kareena Kapoor and television presenter Malaika Khan, as well as the actor Hritik Roshan. The man who says he eventually came up with the idea of Shilpa was Bobby Khan, who has been involved with Bollywood for years. 'The channel was very interested in roping in Hritik Roshan,' he said. 'This was the time when *Dhoom* was about to be released and I told them frankly that they couldn't match his fee. So that was that. Personally I feel SRK [Shahrukh Khan] would have been the best choice, but that was not to be.'

However, he had known Shilpa for a long time and felt she might just be the one. 'Seeing all that is going on in the show, I feel now that Shilpa is the right choice,' he said. 'She is a very mature and level-headed person with absolutely no ego and is very warm and family oriented.'

She was also being given her due back home for the sheer guts she had to appear on the show. 'But despite naysayers who brush her aside as a not-so-happening actress Shilpa must be given credit for stepping out of big, bold secure Bollywood to enter a show where arguably none of her co-stars are even aware of her celebrity status and where most importantly she has to share screen space with temperamental stars,' wrote *City Times*.

As the housemates gathered the following day to discuss which items to order from their luxury shopping list, signs that they really were interested in one another's cultures continued to appear. Jo began telling Shilpa about the various different kinds of curry on offer in England – mushroom bhaji, onion bhaji, poppadom and so on, to the amazement of the latter, who had not realised how different the British version was to what she would have found at home.

Nor had Dirk's ardour cooled: he continued to chase after Shilpa at every opportunity. 'Come and sit on my lap,' he invited her. 'It's the warmest place. I'm not just joking, I'm telling you, where I come from, body heat! When my kids get really cold in the cabin, we all sleep together.'

Shilpa remained goodhearted about it all.

Signs of her changing status, though, began to emerge when the 2007 IIFA (International Indian Film Academy) awards came up for discussion. This is a Bollywood event, which was to be held in Yorkshire, and here just a smidgeon of ego was allowed to emerge: 'That's going to be fantastic, because I think I'll be the only one that's recognised,' she said.

However, her newfound British fame had a drawback, as she swiftly realised. 'I used to leave my country and come here or New York to shop so I wouldn't be disturbed,' she said gloomily. 'Now another country is out of bounds as far as shopping is concerned.'

'Hats, glasses, clothes … nobody would look twice,' Dirk advised her, although it was hard to see Shilpa going for that particular look.

'Baggy trousers … I wouldn't go out looking like a movie or TV star, I would go out looking like a schlub!' Shilpa a schlub? It didn't seem that convincing.

Because Jade's time in the household had been so tumultuous, it was easy to forget that the show still had a way to run before it was through, and so Big Brother continued to set challenges for the housemates. The latest was to answer questions about each other. Someone doing the planning behind the scenes must have had a sense of humour as the person chosen to answer questions about Shilpa was Jack. In the event, he only got one question right – her star sign – while Shilpa herself, who was quizzed about Jermaine, managed three correct answers, which resulted in him getting a pair of shoes.

Incarceration in the house was certainly leading the remaining inmates to divulge all sorts of intimacies they might not have done only a few weeks beforehand. One subject that kept raising its head was lavatory habits, which impelled Shilpa to confess that she took a laxative every night. 'One clearance in the morning and that's it,' she said. 'It will take away all your water retention and everything.'

Jermaine, meanwhile, continued to talk about his own bugbear – food. 'You eat chocolate, potato chips, all kinds of junk,' he remonstrated with Shilpa. 'You eat whatever people put in front of you. Have you ever taken everything you eat and drink in a day and mixed it up and smelled it? You wouldn't believe the smell! That's what's in your stomach.'

It was hardly gripping stuff, but then the inmates had by now been incarcerated for nearly three weeks.

Indeed, intimacies continued to be revealed. Shilpa again mentioned the fact that someone had once wanted to marry her, but that it hadn't worked out, nor had a couple of subsequent relationships. She also put up a spirited defence of arranged marriages. 'I think love is the most overrated emotion on the scale,' she said. 'I believe if two people are compatible and have respect for each other they can work it out. There are so many love marriages that don't work out. There are so many arranged marriages that don't work. What I'm saying is that I don't mind an arranged marriage if I like the guy.'

It was an eminently sensible attitude and one that no doubt her fans will press her on in the future. Back in the house, she cooked dinner (this time with no screaming matches following on immediately afterwards) and they all got going on the next task – to lick giant ice cubes – that would allow them to go to a party that evening. The task was appropriate for it had been snowing outside, something Shilpa appeared ecstatic about.

More silly tasks followed to keep both housemates and viewers amused. One game that the participants genuinely seemed to enjoy involved getting items out of the lounge. Big Brother had turned it into a high-security area, with bars stopping anyone from getting through, and so the contestants were forced to use poles with coat hangers attached to the end. The items they had to retrieve were as varied as they were ridiculous: a fish, some jewellery and a stuffed teddy bear among a good deal else. Much jollity and laughing was involved; earlier tensions seemed to have evaporated.

Dirk swung between some grumpiness and cheeriness, but the latter was now out in full force. In fact, he was sounding positively philosophical. 'Yeah, that's what they all say,' he said, on being told by Shilpa to go to sleep. 'Cool down, just take it easy! Don't get yourself so worked up over nothing. Oh, man, what an adventure – thrown together like this. It's a long way from Bombay to London, it's a long way from curry to crisps. We've been here one moon. I measure everything in moons. It was a full moon when I left and it'll be a full moon when I go home.' Home was clearly what Dirk was beginning to need.

Indeed, everyone now seemed to be in a tetchy mood. Shilpa was uncharacteristically snappy with Jermaine as he hovered in the background while she was cooking and she told him a couple of times to go away. She recovered herself, though, to be able to take part in a conversation about the fact that Ian was gay, adding that gays in India still faced persecution – she was, after all, an AIDS activist. Dirk was in attentive mode; the others were looking as if they were glad the show was finally nearing its end.

With anticipation growing now as never before about who would be the ultimate winner of the show, the last Friday before the winner was to be announced on the Sunday was beset by tensions. For a start, Endemol had been fretting about the future of *Big Brother*, given the number of people who had called for this to be the last series, and so attempted to display contrition and regret before the show even began. It started with a statement – some might say far too little and far too late – 'This series of *Celebrity Big Brother* has divided the nation like never before and we genuinely regret any offence this has caused some people.' Offence was putting it mildly – a diplomatic incident had narrowly been avoided. Clearly, some TV bosses were mightily relieved that the end was finally in sight.

And it wasn't just Endemol who felt they'd better say something. Andy Duncan said, 'There are lessons to be learned from this. There are important creative and tonal challenges about where *Big Brother* goes next.

We can't not take what happened into account in the way in which we think about *Big Brother* 8.'

Just in case anyone thought the next series was going to be bland, however, Andy Duncan did go on to say that there may yet be fresh rows to come. The experience had been 'in one sense good television', he said, adding that it was 'obviously highly controversial, which caused upset to a lot of people ... We very much regretted that.'

Five housemates faced eviction: Shilpa, Jo, Dirk, Ian and Cleo. Only Jack and Danielle, who continued to have attacks of nerves about what sort of reception awaited her outside, knew they were safe. And then, in a quite spectacular error, which merely drew yet more attention to the show, Channel 4 managed to mix up the telephone numbers they'd published on screen, meaning that people who thought they were voting to save Shilpa were, in fact, voting for her eviction. The votes cast to that point were pronounced void and viewers who had rung in were told they would get their money back.

'This was a genuine mistake due to human error,' said a spokesman for Endemol. 'We apologise to viewers and feel the best way to rectify the error is to cancel the vote so far and reopen the voting again.

Shilpa steps into the *Celebrity Big Brother* house. Little did she know that her presence would create an unprecedented media storm.

© Rex Features

Happier times in the house.

Above: Shilpa shares a domestic moment with Dirk Benedict.

Below: Cleo, Dirk, Jermaine, Shilpa and Danielle perform their winning number as the Jackson Five.

Above: Jade has no trouble expressing her opinions about Shilpa and, *below*, Shilpa's dismayed reaction.

© *Rex Features*

A reconciliation – but how much of it was for the benefit of the cameras?

Above: Danielle Lloyd laughs during an argument between Jade and Shilpa.

© Rex Features

Below: Did the contestants inside the house realise quite how much of a media frenzy they were whipping up in the big wide world?

© Empics

She's out! Shilpa emerges as the winner with her characteristic poise and dignity.
© David Mepham/WENN

Shilpa's parents, Sunanda and Surendra, pose at the family home in the midst of the media furore. Sunanda said she always knew that Shilpa was going to be special.

Shilpa, looking
exquisite and
composed, waits to
be interviewed by
Kay Burley for
Sky Television.
© Rex Features

Viewers who voted can have a full refund and any unclaimed monies will be donated to charity.'

Channel 4 was equally embarrassed. 'There was an error in the on-screen information about Friday night's eviction vote in relation to the eviction phone line details for Shilpa,' said a spokesman. 'While the voice-over was correct and stated "to vote to evict Shilpa" the on-screen text mistakenly read "to vote to save Shilpa".'

This created a mini furore in itself, although it died down rather more quickly than the previous row about racism.

In the event, the next two people to be evicted were Jo and Cleo. The audience was back – the duo left to a mixture of cheers and boos – but there was still no live press conference afterwards; the whole matter was still highly sensitive and Channel 4 was taking no risks.

Danielle, yet again, broke down. Once more Shilpa comforted her. Everyone was at sixes and sevens, and with the end now in sight, an end some people were also dreading, emotions ran high. 'As you see people getting out of the house, it's the strangest emotion I've ever come across – of happiness and sadness, and so much confusion,' was how Shilpa herself put it in the Diary Room.

Perhaps Danielle was so upset because she belatedly remembered the advice her agent had given her before she went in. An e-mail had come to light in which her agent, Angela de Fouw, had given her some very good advice about how to conduct herself within the house, advice that she appeared to have forgotten.

The 'Do' list said:

- Be yourself – natural, down to earth; if you've got something to say, say it to someone's face.

- Join in when asked to do tasks, get your hands dirty (not literally!). Show you're game for a laugh.

- Introduce yourself when you go in, Hi, I'm Danielle Lloyd, you may know me from the beauty pageant world, etc. Some may not know who you are.

- Be interested in others. Show you want to find out about them. But do it naturally, of course.

- It mustn't seem forced or artificial but try to include a comment about something that's newsworthy each day. Those comments might make the papers.

- Be kind. For example, if someone's being bullied and you don't agree, stick up for him or her. Be a mate!

- Remember how *I'm A Celeb* changed people's perception of Jordan.

To say that her comments might make the papers and that she should be a mate seemed more than a little to the point: as with Jade, it was now possible to feel something approaching pity for Danielle.

The 'Don't' list was equally striking:

- Don't whisper – your mic will pick it up. If your face is on screen, TV crew will lip-read. If you think you'll regret saying/doing something, don't say/do it.
- Don't get stuck with the glamour girls (if there are any), they'll encourage you to be bitchy maybe. Show there's much more to you than a face and body.
- Don't be racist – show you're bigger than that. If you have a strong opinion about something, give your reasons for it.
- Don't put yourself in situations where it looks like you're flirting with men. That links in with your morals.
- Don't talk about Teddy all the time, people will get bored.
- Don't do anything that could be seen as 'cheating'. Press will be looking for something like that.
- Refer to your website but don't say the name – they'll find it.

- Try not to have a cob on, or, if you are grumpy, say why, e.g. I'm bloody tired, hungry, etc.

It was all good advice, to be sure.

Outside, Cleo was keen to talk about Dirk: he, it seemed, was the housemate who most annoyed her, given that he had mood swings – one day grumpy and the next cheery and in pursuit of Shilpa again. 'I could have murdered him,' she said. 'At the same time I understand that we're under a lot of pressure. He comes out and you think Dirk's arrived. He arrived in those moments and then he goes back to being grumpy and growly, and smoking cigars in the kitchen and we exercised a lot of tolerance – he did push it. [But] now we are huge chums. The one thing I'm glad of is being in the house you have to stay in there and see things through. He admitted to playing games, he admitted to lying, he admitted to messing.'

As for who would be the ultimate winner, Cleo – who was as yet unaware of quite the extent of the furore of recent weeks – thought it would be the erstwhile member of The Jackson Five. 'If someone's going to win with honour and respect, and everything that would show what a great accolade the *Big Brother* house is, it should be Jermaine,' she said. 'Without Jermaine I wouldn't be here right now. He's a wonderful good man and we could all learn from Jermaine.'

All of this was listened to with due solemnity, but the real curiosity value, of course, lay in what Jo had to say. Unlike Jade – or perhaps not fully understanding the seriousness of the situation – she was defiant. 'I didn't never mean it in that way,' she protested on being shown the footage that had shocked the world. 'I'm not a racist, I know that I'm not!'

To emphasise the extent of the controversy, Jo was then shown footage of the headlines and demonstrations that had taken place across the world. 'Oh my God,' she said, and added, 'It does look very bad. [But] I am not a racist person at all. My cousin is married to an Indian man, and my cousins are half-Indian.'

What about mocking Shilpa's background? 'I didn't even know I was doing it.'

Had she encouraged Jade? 'I didn't mean to, if I did.'

Nor, she said, did she dislike Shilpa. 'I'm not going to deny that Shilpa did aggravate me a lot – you can't click with everybody you meet,' she said. 'It's not because I'm racist at all. I think she's a very beautiful, very elegant woman.'

On mimicking Shilpa's accent, she said, 'We was doing that with her and she was finding that really funny. I didn't never mean it in that way – I didn't even know I was doing it. It wasn't a personal attack at all.'

Cleo, at least, was delighted to be free once more. She had emerged from the show with a good deal of credit, not only for not having joined in the nastiness, but also for trying to keep Shilpa's spirits up. And she revealed quite how strange conditions in the house were – something the viewers would never have been aware of. 'I went for my first walk, which I know sounds bizarre, but my legs have been like jelly,' she said, when asked what she had been doing since leaving the house. 'We don't use our legs in there very much, so to go for a walk is very strange and a bit trembly.'

Cleo was also recognised everywhere she went. 'I went up to our local supermarket with my mum and the reaction has been really lovely,' she said. 'Everyone from everywhere and every age has been really lovely, and when you are in there you feel like you have been put in a shoebox at the back of the attic and everyone has left the country so it's a real surprise actually. It feels strange that people have actually been watching.'

And it had certainly taken its toll. Cleo was being extremely diplomatic about the whole thing, but her relief at being away from it all was palpable. 'For me the whole experience in the house was not at all what I expected and I had the most dreadful nervous stomach from the beginning to end,' she admitted. 'The one good thing is that I have lost a lot of weight, which has been fabulous – the *Big Brother* diet. I thought it would be a lot more fun. I didn't enjoy it in a fun kind of way. I enjoyed meeting everyone, I loved Jermaine, I loved everyone that I met in there.'

Jermaine clearly had made a big impression on her, for he provided Cleo with the best moment in the house. 'Being in The Jackson Five with Jermaine teaching it, that was just the best,' she said. 'That was great. The water fight one night in the bathroom and I couldn't stop laughing – that was good. And the last task where you had to rescue things from the front room, that was lots of fun.'

However, as the world now knows, there was a downside, and, asked what had shocked her most, Cleo replied, 'I would have to say the conversations with Danielle. In there, we all thought she is going to win because in there she is a happy young pony. Then you suddenly see the other conversations that are going on and you're just like "Wow!" I had no idea what was going on in the house I was living in.'

Back in the house, the controversy was far from over. Yet another race row erupted, this one started by Dirk, of all people. It all began because Shilpa asked him, 'How many [Indians] are there here?'

His answer, given what had gone before, was a little tactless. 'Oh millions, millions,' he replied. 'And they're breeding fast. The demographics [of Britain] are changing. I think the average British woman has 1.3 children and the average Indian has three. So they're taking over. There'll be Nehru as a prime minister, a Gandhi.'

Shilpa's response was to put her head in her hands, before telling the Diary Room the next day that *Big Brother* 'has affected me in a very positive way. It doesn't matter what country you're from, we're all the same, we're human.'

It must be said that it didn't look as if Dirk had the faintest idea he might be causing offence. The remarks came off the top of his head, and clearly he was being flippant. Nor did he imply that it would be any bad thing to have a Nehru or Gandhi as prime minister. But such was the heated awareness about racial matters in the wake of all that had gone before that his remarks were seized upon as further proof of the real attitudes held by the West. Some people felt that he thought Indians would take over because they were 'breeding like rabbits rather than because they are any good, have talent or ability'. Others merely took it as a sign of innate prejudice. It was certainly a remark that was given a good deal more attention than it deserved.

The next day dawned, the penultimate one in the house. The contestants were woken up, appropriately enough, to the sound of Frank Sinatra singing 'My Way'. The atmosphere was a mixture of tension and hilarity: there was much screaming and jousting as various housemates waxed one another's bodies. Meanwhile, viewers had been sending questions into the house.

Shilpa, of course, was by this time of particular interest, and she was asked, 'Shilpa, as a celeb, what prompted you to do this and how has it affected you?'

This question was more loaded with meaning than Shilpa could possibly have realised. Outside, interest in the housemates and the outcome of the show was at fever pitch with the various controversies it had thrown up showing no sign of dying down. In the event, Shilpa (rather immodestly) said that she had gone on the show because she'd always been a trendsetter. She continued, 'It has given me the opportunity to understand myself and also understand the fact it doesn't matter which country you belong to, we are all human and we all share the same emotions. And how has it affected me? I'm brain dead! I think it's given me the opportunity to understand myself. And that it doesn't matter what country you're from, we're all human and all share the same emotions.'

It was a sentiment that couldn't be faulted and touched on exactly what had caused such outrage in the outside world.

But there was still time to fill, and another *Big Brother* task was at hand. The housemates were asked to act out their most memorable moments in the house, the catch being that they couldn't play themselves. Shilpa ended up as Danielle!

6
And the Winner Is ...

The day finally dawned: it was Sunday, 28 January, and the most controversial series ever of *Big Brother* was about to come to a close. There were six housemates left in situ – Shilpa, Jermaine, Dirk, Ian, Danielle and Jack – and, no matter how cool they tried to be, nerves kept showing through.

'Last day! I thought it'd never come,' said Ian.

'I had the worst sleep in 25 days,' said Shilpa. 'Are you happy?'

'I'm ecstatic!' cried Ian. 'Over the moon, just don't know what I'm going out to. I'm going to miss you.'

'You too,' said Shilpa.

But the ordeal was not yet quite over. After waking to the strains of 'Never Forget' by Take That – as if! – the housemates were set their penultimate task: to set up a row of dominoes throughout the house and then topple them all in one flowing movement.

Mission accomplished, they were given a hamper including lip gloss and face cream (for men). Shilpa and Ian seemed particularly excited about the contents and spent a happy time together putting on make-up.

Their final task, appropriately for a show such as *Big Brother*, was to participate in a game of 'Simon Says'. 'Big Brother says, put your hands in the air,' intoned Big Brother, and the only one not to do so was Shilpa, who was promptly kicked out.

By this stage, though, nothing much seemed to matter any more. The housemates were indulging in some hilarity, almost certainly caused by increasing nerves: the moment they had all been waiting for was nearly upon them. For Shilpa, a spectacular gamble was about to pay off.

Not that she was taking anything for granted. 'Each one of us in this house deserves to win it. If I win it, it will be God's grace, my destiny and the audience's love,' she declared before the final result was announced. 'I don't want to think about it because they say expectation is the root cause of all sorrow. So I don't want to expect it and then be sad. If it happens, it happens, and if it doesn't, it's OK.'

Given the furore, subsequent apologies and delicacy surrounding the situation, unusually but understandably, neither Jade nor Jo was present to see the finale. All the other housemates were there, though, and the first two to be evicted were Danielle and Jack. The former, in particular, had in the past seemed petrified by what awaited her, but now she seemed quite composed: 'It's OK,' she told everyone else.

As Danielle and Jack left the house, a chorus of boos greeted them. 'Quite a heavy atmosphere there,' said Davina briskly, before losing no time in showing the duo the clips that had caused so much outrage and offence. In particular, Danielle was shown the shot of her saying Shilpa should 'fuck off back home'.

'It was said in the heat of the moment,' said a nervous Danielle. 'Everyone's arguing and I've ... I don't know, it just came out.'

And why had she been laughing as Shilpa and Jade fought? 'I hate confrontation,' she said. 'I wasn't laughing at Shilpa, it was just nerves. I hate confrontation – it was just a natural reaction.'

Danielle pointed out that things changed after Jade

left the house. 'Since Jade went, I spoke to Shilpa and got on with her,' she said, before saying that she thought Shilpa would be understanding when shown the clips of the others bad-mouthing her behind her back (lucky for Danielle, she was). 'I have learned not to be such a bitch,' she admitted.

Jack was also adamant he was not a racist. 'I'm completely shocked,' he said. 'I didn't like her to begin with. I'm allowed to not like her, it was nothing to do with the colour of her skin or where she's from. It was the squeaky voice just annoyed me. I like her now. In the Diary Room I said, "She's a sweet girl." In the end I really liked her.'

Astonishingly, Jo remained defiant. Despite the fact that she was now well aware of the enormity of the scandal, she declared she still had no regrets. 'I've been accused of mocking Shilpa's accent, but that is not racist,' she said.

'My cousin married an Indian and I make fun of their kids' voices. Then they make funny Cockney noises back at me. It's just a big game. I can't say I am sorry for something I am not guilty of. If I went back in there, then I'd say it all again.'

Next to leave the house was Ian, who bounded down the steps crying, 'Oh, Davina, oh, Davina!' Indeed, he seemed quite overwhelmed. 'I didn't think I would be in the final,' he said. 'I gave myself two weeks and I didn't think I would last any longer.'

Like the others, he was flabbergasted both at the scenes of bullying and the international response it had provoked. 'I actually didn't feel comfortable or equipped to deal with that situation,' he said. 'I completely back away from conflict and Jermaine was there to save the day. I strongly disagreed with one side of the argument.

'I didn't agree with what Jade was saying. I love Shilpa to bits and I don't think she has a bad bone in her body. There was nothing fuelled from racism whatsoever. It was just magnified and petty and blown out of proportion. I really felt a lot more relaxed the last week. Being in the middle of it, I don't like conflict at all.'

Inside the house, tensions were mounting. It was now between Shilpa, Dirk and Jermaine, and, while to the outside viewer, who had been aware of what had been going on, it was probably pretty obvious who was going to win, the three inside had no such insight.

It was finally Dirk who got the call – and who told Big Brother to wait a moment, as he was hugging Shilpa, saying, 'You poor kids, I will see you later' –

and who emerged to tremendous cheers. The crowd outside was singing the theme tune to *The A-Team*, and, with immense good humour, he joined in. He liked Shilpa, all right, he confessed, but she dumped him 'in the second week'. 'I made a good run at it,' he continued. 'I tried.'

As for the nastiness, not only had he not been implicated but he was hardly aware of what had gone on. 'I was out in the garden,' he said. 'I didn't move, I didn't do a lot of separating. She's [Shilpa's] elegant, she's sweet, she's adaptable and she's got a great sense of humour.'

In many ways, Jermaine was overshadowed by what came next, as, after it was announced that he was the runner-up, the real focus almost immediately centred on the winner, Shilpa, who looked as if she couldn't quite believe her ears, before she screamed and began to cry. Jermaine comforted her with good grace, although it was not clear if either realised quite what a nail-biter this series had turned out to be. 'Kindness is a strength,' he said, and then headed for the door.

Jermaine was a deserving runner-up. At times he had seemed almost the only voice of sanity in the house and he certainly disapproved strongly of the bullying and shrieking that had gone on. When the nastiness was at its height, he had spoken out. 'The other girls were laughing. They are being controlled by Jade; it's ignorance,' he said. 'You can't reason with stupidity ... Look at the song "Man in The Mirror",' he said of the three girls. 'They need to look in the mirror before they can make that change.'

However, like Shilpa, he refused to condemn Jade outright. Clearly, he realised she was a victim of her own background and, like Shilpa, he did not want her demonised. 'I happen to like Jade,' he said. 'She is who she is, but Shilpa is from another culture and they did not fit.'

The housemates all obviously loved him, not least because of what was probably his most famous moment, on day 17. 'When I'm gone, I'm going to miss everyone because my love is real,' he said. 'I'm one way, I just wanted to say that.'

There are plenty of people who believe *Celebrity Big Brother* is a very good way of showing up someone's real character and, if that is the case, Jermaine, for one, should be proud.

Shilpa had won 67 per cent of the vote, and the show's prize of £100,000, but, above all, of course, she had proved herself able to rise above a nasty situation, kept her dignity and been a credit to her country. Britain also felt it had redeemed itself when she got such a decisive win.

And, of course, there was the fact that Shilpa had gone from being a complete unknown to a woman with a massive profile in the West, with untold opportunities opening out before her. For her, this was an extraordinary step forward, a massive gamble that had comprehensively paid off.

After Jermaine left, Shilpa – clad in a magnificent red silk top – was left on her own until the call finally came. To cheers from the crowds, she appeared, waving and looking both excited and overwhelmed.

Then, for the first time, she saw what the others had been saying behind her back. The exchange between Shilpa and Davina went as follows:

'What was it like waiting in there on your own?' Davina began.

'I was in shock,' said Shilpa. 'I was in shock.' At this point she broke off to shout to the cheering and screaming crowd, 'Chicken curry rules!'

'Shilpa, you've been on such a journey in that house,' continued Davina. 'What's it been like for you?'

'Oh, tell me about it,' said Shilpa, looking radiant. 'I don't want to sound clichéd but it's truly been quite a roller coaster. The highs, the lows ... [it] taught me so, so much.'

'From where you've come from and the kind of lifestyle you lead, being thrown into that house must have been a shock,' commented Davina. 'What was the biggest shock for you, domestically?'

'Oh, to cook!' Shilpa cried.

'I can see!' said Davina. 'On a more serious note, it was one of your downs that caused a complete furore here on the outside. It's been an international incident – have you got any idea what that could be?'

'Really?' asked Shilpa. 'I have no idea what's been happening on the outside. We didn't even have a real lawn, we had plastic grass!'

'So you've got no idea what this enormous controversy could be about?' asked Davina.

'I have an inkling but I'd love to hear some news,' Shilpa replied.

And, with that, *Big Brother* began to show footage of the rows that had gone on in the house, centring, of course, on the racism. Much of it was new to Shilpa, as it had been said behind her back, and she was quite visibly upset.

'That's quite heavy, watching that back, because obviously you weren't privy to a lot of what was said,'

said Davina, the master of the understatement. 'How are you feeling?'

'I just want to forget things,' said Shilpa, who was on the verge of tears, before going on to show all the forgiveness that had won her so many fans. 'Things happen and people make mistakes. We're all human beings, we're all fallible.

'Jade didn't mean to be racist. If this created any sort of misunderstanding, I want to put things to rest – she is not a racist. I am so happy I took up this opportunity. I don't want people to think [they] welcomed an Indian and she made trouble here.'

'After that speech, I'm not sure if this is the right word, this magna… mangnamanity [sic]?' asked Davina. 'Shilpa, you understand what I'm trying to say? After that, I think that is why you are sat there. You are a very forgiving and loving person. You've said it all in a nutshell. Let's move forward, past the argument, to happier times. How do you think you've changed?'

'Whoah!' said Shilpa, cheering up. 'My mother will be in for such a huge shock. She never, never has not been around when I've achieved something – travelled. This is the first time in my life I've done something on my own and I've never won anything in my life. I was rejected as a model; before that I entered some stupid competition, Netru, Indru, Naalai, I lost even that!'

'Listen, quickfire questions for you,' said Davina. 'This is a very important one, yes. What would it take for Dirk to win you over?'

'Oh, well, he'd have to be 38 years younger and start eating chicken and move to India, or England,' she replied.

'The young thing is an issue, though – we can't ever make him younger,' said Davina. 'Can you sum up your experience in three words?'

'In three words: Incredible, overwhelming ... chicken curry rules!' cried Shilpa.

'Shilpa, you have been through your ups and downs, you really have, but never knowingly without a knockout pair of earrings,' Davina remarked. 'Here's the story of your time in the house ...'

And, with that, footage of Shilpa in the house was played. She eventually left, into the waiting arms of her mother. Good had triumphed, the bullies had been sent off in disgrace and the most controversial series ever of *Big Brother* was finally at an end.

The sense of relief among the great and good was palpable. For a short time, it had looked as if a bunch of silly girls was going to tar the whole nation with their brush, but this result showed that Britain really was a modern country at ease with itself, ready to show a welcoming face to the world.

Others were only too keen to highlight what had been going on, however, and foremost among these was Trevor Phillips, chair of the Commission For Equality And Human Rights. He said, 'It's great Shilpa made it all the way to the final. We haven't yet defeated racism in our country but last night's vote shows that we are determined to beat the scourge of bigotry and to drive prejudice from our shores. We should be congratulating Shilpa. It has taken a woman from a former colony, thousands of miles away, to remind us of what we most value about being British.'

He wasn't the only one to speak out, and there were quite a few people not willing to let Channel 4 off the hook that lightly. 'It is indeed good that the show has raised the issue of racism,' said Birmingham Labour MP Khalid Mahmood. 'But it has left a bad taste. People in the UK are the most tolerant in Europe on race issues and I think that needs to be reflected.'

And the British government, in some form or another, was determined to get its oar in. The lucky man who got to speak out was education secretary Alan Johnson, who said that *Big Brother* had 'hammered home' the need for teenagers to be taught 'British values'.

'The current debate has been good in one way – it has highlighted the need to make sure schools focus on the core British values of justice and tolerance,' he went on. 'We want the world to be talking about the respect and understanding we give all cultures, not the ignorance and bigotry shown on our TV screens.'

But this was not just the government shouldering its way to the forefront: the row had affected so many people and raised so many sensitivities that quite a few people felt really compelled to speak out. '*Celebrity Big Brother* has allowed us to discuss and explore the low-level racism that floats around in our society,' said Shiraz Chakera of the General Teaching Council for England. 'We should do more to tackle the problem in schools and teach children to rise above the problem.'

Even religious leaders entered the fray. 'This *Big Brother* row has exposed an ugly underbelly in society,' said the Archbishop of York John Sentamu. 'It has highlighted how people are only too ready to point the finger at the foreigner, or those who might not fit in. Shilpa showed remarkable grace in how she reacted to bullying. She dealt with it well.'

She most certainly did, and she continued to do so, too. Whether it was because of an innate sweetness, or simply because she realised it was best to move on, Shilpa appeared almost saintly in her forgiveness and her pleas that everyone else should forgive Jade, Danielle and Jo, too. 'They are young, but not racist,' she said, and that was just about the wisest thing she could have said at that juncture.

Danielle herself was appalled by what she'd done. Having lost a modelling contract and with rumours her relationship with Teddy Sheringham was on the rocks, she could not do enough to make up for what she had said. She too made a statement to the press the morning after the night before.

'Yeah, I'd like to apologise to everybody for the words that I have said,' she remarked. 'They were never, ever, ever meant in a racist way whatsoever. And I'm not a racist. I think Shilpa's a fantastic, beautiful lady, and I'm very, very sorry, Shilpa.'

'I just want to say, whatever happened, I don't really want to blame anyone, especially not Danielle,' said Shilpa, who again looked close to tears. 'I saw the footage for the first time – it was ghastly. But now I just want to move forward in life. Jade Goody is not a bad person. She is just young – people are fallible. So there is nothing in my heart, the day we hugged, it was all gone and forgotten, really.

'She is a mother of two and I do not want to see her ruined because of this. It was just a game, we played that game and now it is over. I just want to thank them for all their support and I'm very proud to be an Indian and very proud of my colour. And I just want them to know there is no reason to feel what they feel as long as you carry yourself well with dignity; with kindness in your heart, it can never go wrong.

'So it really doesn't matter what people think of you and perceive of you. I think everything in the *Big Brother* house is really magnified. I just want them to understand that it was just a game. It's over; it's out of the way. Let's move on.'

With an attitude like that, Shilpa won over even more fans than before. Nor was she exactly short of offers: world famous, internationally recognised and with a sweet nature, too, the world was hers for the taking. While she was still inside the house, her mother Sunanda had signed up with the master of the game: she was in talks with Max Clifford about how they were going to take it from there.

'She certainly has a great deal of offers already on

the table,' Clifford said. 'What we now have to discuss is exactly what she wants to do. I will be sitting down with Shilpa and her mother very soon. The emphasis will certainly be on quality rather than quantity but there is interest from television and film.

'I think she handled herself excellently while she was in the house. By forgiving her fellow housemates and talking about how she thinks their comments were based on ignorance rather than racism, she has taken a huge step.'

Of course, back in India, people were jubilant. The press there had been following matters as closely as they had done in the UK, and they, too, deemed Shilpa to have been a credit to her country. Britain had also come good at last.

'Britain is a tolerant nation despite the vile scenes which caused outrage,' said ExpressIndia.com, while one blog poster said, 'Looks like the whole of Britain took upon itself the onerous responsibility to gainsay whatever Jade said. And that saw Shilpa winning the race. Well done, Britain. You are truly civilised.'

The Times of India, which had also been closely following events, and had set up a mini-website to report on *Big Brother*, was thoughtful in its reaction to the news. '*Big Brother* has unwittingly done the

British society a favour by exposing the issue of racism,' it reported.

'Because it happened on live TV, it is suddenly OK to talk about it openly (both for and against it) and the British do not shy away from holding their own faults under the lens so hopefully this would lead to a more thorough self-examination of the issues of equality and acceptance for all within Britain.'

It must be said that not everyone on the Indian sub-continent was treating *Big Brother* as if it had been a major world event. Indeed, on the street many Indians seemed rather bemused by the whole furore, to say nothing of being a little bit curious as to why Shilpa had agreed to take part.

But on the whole they were fairly proud. Public relations executive Perizaad Mistree told the BBC news website that she was 'very happy and proud' that Shilpa had won. 'It's good for her that, in spite of nasty things happening to her, she held on and emerged a winner. I am really happy for her,' she said.

It was interesting, too, to see that some Indians were convinced that the racism row had very much helped Shilpa to win – nor were they particularly impressed that it was she who had gone on the programme rather than a much bigger star.

'Who knows Shilpa Shetty otherwise?' asked Hiral Chheda, a housewife who had been watching the programme. 'We are not talking about a Kareena Kapoor or Rani Mukherjee here. In the end, however, so long as you are making a name and money out of it, any publicity is good. I am happy that she has won but it's not like she's got medals for the country, you know.'

Film director Shyam Benegal commented, 'I am happy, delighted that she has won. [But] I am not sure she would have won had it not been for the media attention she got then. In any case, such programmes thrive on media hype.'

Nor was he certain that it would help her in her Bollywood career. 'It's difficult to say because Indian audiences behave in an insular manner and rarely get affected by what happens abroad,' he said. 'She has certainly gotten offers in the UK and one hears of projects coming her way so she is definitely looking at a vibrant new career.'

But there were sceptics too. 'She should not feel happy about winning a cheap television show, this is no accomplishment,' said Aftab Alam, a banker, adding that Shilpa should really be concentrating on her career back in India.

Not that she needed to be unduly concerned. By the

time she had been out of the house for two days, estimates about her future earning power had risen to the £10 million mark, which was not an unrealistic amount. Given that Jade herself had earned between £4 million and £8 million, depending on who you believed, Shilpa, with far greater potential, was clearly capable of earning a great deal more.

According to others, even if she didn't want to cash in on her increased earning potential, she had enhanced not only her career prospects, but also her romantic ones. It was said that Sunanda was aware of the possibility of finding a British-based Indian magnate for her daughter to marry – after all, in the West these days, 31 is no age at all.

'Sunanda is of the opinion that Shilpa has already left it too late and must act fast, capitalising on her appeal if she wants to find a man,' said a friend. 'Sunanda has flown over with the express purpose of finding Shilpa a suitable husband – someone who is very wealthy and of Indian descent who will seal the family's future wealth.'

And so the options appeared to be £10 million earnings or a wealthy husband. The future couldn't have looked rosier.

7
Outside the House

Since leaving the house, Shilpa hadn't put a foot wrong. Her grace and presence had already won her an army of fans in situ and, now outside, her popularity was rocketing almost by the minute. Offers flooded in and it was clear that a new and shining future awaited her. For the first time, she had been exposed to the full footage of what had happened in the house to her face and behind her back. While she had been shocked by the snippets Davina had shown her, it was nothing compared to how she felt when she saw the reality of what had gone on. Plainly shocked, she talked to the *Daily Mirror* at length about what had happened and what she now felt about her time in the *Celebrity Big Brother* house.

'I'd no idea it was so bad,' admitted a stunned Shilpa, as she watched Jade, Jo and, alas, Danielle hurling insults behind her back. In the cold light of day it appeared even worse than when it was first shown on television and her hurt was palpable. 'I didn't know all that had gone on,' she said. 'They are so mean. Why didn't someone stop them? It hurts me deeply. Look at me ... I am shaking.'

The first footage she saw was the bitching and abuse after the Oxo cube incident. If ever a situation had been allowed to get out of control, this was it, and, given the trivial thing it had stemmed from, it seemed utterly extraordinary in the cold light of day. Jade was shown at her absolute foul-mouthed worst, screaming that Shilpa was a 'fucking wanker', a 'fucking liar' and a 'fake', amid a good deal else. No one would have enjoyed hearing this about themselves but for a chaste Indian woman brought up to behave modestly, it was like watching a horror show. Shilpa was appalled. 'Watching this now, I can understand why people complained so much,' she said. 'It isn't just one or two attacks – it's incessant. I still can't figure out what I did wrong.

'Why is there so much hate about an Oxo cube? This is so petty, so juvenile, so nasty ... There is hatred there, and that hurts deeply. Only now, this is sinking in. I am someone who has never been judgemental, but Jade's behaviour is obnoxious, very aggressive, nasty and suffocating. You can see in my body language how much it has hurt me. I'm sorry my family and their families had to see this. My mum said she was worried I was going to be attacked, and now I can see why.'

This was the first time Shilpa had been really critical of Jade, but it was also the first time she was exposed to the full truth about what had been going on. Her attitude, however, remained essentially one of forgiveness – that Jade was to be pitied and shown that her way of thinking was wrong.

As this was happening, Jade had checked into The Priory suffering from severe depression – the consequences of her actions continued to hit home. Meanwhile, Shilpa watched yet more debasement and vulgarity on screen as, deeply upset, she realised that Jo and Danielle were lapping it up. Given that she had become friendly with Danielle, it must have been doubly hurtful to hear her say, 'That was fucking fantastic! That made my day.'

'Why are they laughing?' asked a bewildered Shilpa. 'Why did no one step in to help? What had I done that was so wrong?'

'She can't even speak English properly,' snarled Danielle on screen.

'I speak ten languages and I think my English is fantastic,' snorted Shilpa, watching. 'Can you believe this is the epitome of womanhood? I can't believe women will act like that. It's totally alien to me.'

And a final venomous snap from Danielle: 'I wish she would fuck off home!'

It was almost too much to bear. 'I really don't know why I was singled out for such hatred,' said Shilpa, but she endeavoured, as always, to be fair to the other women. 'Jade has had a tough upbringing but because she made her name on *Big Brother* she was perhaps jealous that I was diverting some of the attention away from her,' she told the *Mirror* (and she may well have been spot on). 'I can see that Jade tried to intimidate me, tried to bully me, but I wouldn't succumb. Maybe that's why I annoyed her so much. I can see that she was playing up to the cameras and Jo and Danielle were egging her on. Jo is perhaps driven by jealousy because she has self-esteem issues. Danielle, well, she is just young and more stupid than racist.

'I'm not excusing what they did, not for a minute. I can see why people felt they had to stick up for me and am grateful for that. And I am proud that Asian people,

Hindus, Sikhs and Muslims have come together. What those girls did was wrong but I would not like to say they are racist. I forgive them because I must. We are all human beings, we all make mistakes – I make plenty of them. What is said is in the past and I don't want to dwell on it because it is too horrid.'

It was exactly the right attitude to take. Also, presumably very much to the relief of Endemol and Channel 4 bosses, Shilpa resolutely stuck to the line that what happened was not racist abuse. She did, however, allow herself some small praise for putting up with it all, as well she might, as well as displaying knowledge of Britain's cultural heritage that might have been unknown to the other women there.

'But when I see the conflict played back, I must say I think I did pretty well,' she remarked. 'I didn't demean myself by using horrible language like the others – there is no need to in the country that brought us William Shakespeare. I kept my dignity. But please, I don't want to see those tapes ever again.'

As for Jade, she was certainly paying the price. Her spokeswoman revealed she was suffering from stress and depression: 'Jade is receiving treatment because she hasn't been sleeping or eating properly. She saw a doctor and he advised that she needed further treatment.' Her mooted trip to India had been cancelled, too. For Jade, it was not a happy state of affairs.

But Shilpa continued to insist – almost certainly rightly – that there was nothing racist about the ordeal she had endured: it was nasty, vindictive bullying, but no more than that. Or, as she put it, it was a fight of right versus wrong. 'And right won. It was not a battle between brown and white, it was a battle between right and wrong – and right won.'

She also kept to her mantra of forgiveness, which must have been hard for the women, if they were capable of thinking about anyone other than themselves at that point, to bear. 'Jade and Jo need professional help, not condemnation,' said Shilpa. 'I am someone who believes in karma ... what you have sowed will be repaid. Maybe Jo is here for what she's done before, maybe she has insecurities because she hasn't achieved all she wanted to in her career. She's become a cynic. I believe in the philosophy that you put the other cheek forward. My parents always called me naive. Jo and I never really bonded on that level and I forgive her as I think she is very low on self-esteem and I just think Jo and Danielle were led.'

Shilpa also seemed to retain a genuine fondness for Danielle, despite what she had just seen. It might not have been much fun for Danielle to hear it, but Shilpa's view was clearly that Danielle wasn't the sharpest pencil in the box and that is what had led her to behave in the way that she did. Indeed, she had even been rooting for her to win. 'Danielle, I'm still OK with,' she told the *Mirror*. 'What she did was horrible and upsetting, but she's very young and stupid. I wanted Danielle to win because it would help with her self-confidence. I don't blame Danielle as much. It was so apparent who started the rift: Jade. I don't think she did it consciously but it was to make sure she didn't get nominated by the girls.'

Shilpa was showing insights into human nature which would have done anyone proud, but one person she did seem to find it difficult to talk nicely about was Jackiey, Jade's mother. Jackiey, of course, had been the one who kept referring to her as 'the Indian' and, unlike the others, did not have the excuse of youth on her side. 'She made me cry,' said Shilpa matter of factly. 'I didn't know where it stemmed from, I didn't do anything to upset her. It was a nightmare. She completely broke me from within. She could have even called me "S" [for Shilpa] if that was easier. But I don't hold it against her. With due respect, she's not all there. I hadn't been doing anything wrong. If I wasn't such a strong person, I would have been a nervous wreck by now.'

And it emerged that there were moments when she had thought of following the example of the three men at the beginning and simply walking out of the show. 'There were times when I did want to leave,' Shilpa revealed. 'I went to my bed and I thought about leaving. Then I saw the photographs of my parents. My mother had told me, "Don't leave the *Big Brother* house a loser, get evicted but don't give up." I've always put up a great fight and I didn't want to go that way.'

Of course, the racism issue kept raising its head, and Shilpa also revealed that it had come up for discussion within the house. Mid Oxo-gate, Jade had said to her, 'Go back to the slums!' which, Shilpa told Cleo, was a 'spur of the moment reaction. It wasn't contrived to be racist. I don't want to perceive it that way. I felt maybe, maybe not,' she said. 'The reason I changed my mind and said she wasn't racist was that I slept on it. It was just really hurtful, I was hurting continually. I woke up every day and saw the pictures of Jade's kids and Cleo kept saying to me, "She's not racist, she's a mum." I had then had time to think about it.'

But the r-word had occurred to others in the house,

too. One who probably knew more about it than anyone else was Jermaine Jackson. As well as trying to look after Shilpa, he also alerted her to what might be going on.

'It was Jermaine who put the thought into my mind,' said Shilpa. 'He said, "Just look at your colour," and I thought, "Could it be?" I'm someone who is an escapist, I was in denial for a very long time. Before Jade arrived, the girls loved my food, then the same girls who loved it started to hate it. But I was first aware of the real strength of their feeling after the argument about the Oxo cubes. It was frightening. I can see why my mum thought I was going to be attacked.

'I thought it was really petty. I stand by the fact that what she did was terrible but I want to believe it wasn't racist. I think it was more jealousy than racism. For example, Danielle had seen that the attention she was getting was diluted. It was a clash of cultures. Jermaine was dragging me away and I am glad he did as I could have said something I regretted. I'm so glad that my parents taught me how to hold my tongue.'

She had indeed acquitted herself with dignity in the most trying of circumstances and it was ironic, in some ways, that racism had come to the centre of the public's attention, as that sort of bullying, whatever form it takes, is horrible to endure. As it was, it resembled nothing so much as a pack of girls in the common room, spitefully picking on someone cleverer, prettier and more able than they are.

'It suddenly sunk in [that] they just don't like me,' revealed Shilpa, in the interview. 'It just felt terrible. I was worried but I wasn't intimidated. They tried to bully me. They started to gang up on me because I wasn't going to be part of their clique. They were doing lots of things I couldn't associate myself with.'

Indeed, it was notable that it was the Brits disgracing themselves, while the guests on these shores behaved considerably better. A certain amount of burping and farting went on – indeed, even Jermaine complained about Jackiey – which, to a well-brought-up girl from India, must have been an agony to endure.

'I couldn't believe it, all the burping and flatulence. It was like nothing I had ever seen or heard before. Jermaine, Dirk and I felt uncool for not burping and farting. But I couldn't ask them to stop because that's not me. The bathroom was horrible, it was kind of unsanitary. We had one bathroom and one toilet between all of us. I cleaned it once, Dirk did it twice and Cleo did it once. But I don't think I saw Jo even wash her cup.'

And Shilpa confirmed that some of the housemates had suspected some of what was going on outside. It was after helicopters came near the house that the housemates began to realise something might be wrong, and, after one of them spent time in the Diary Room, her demeanour seemed to change. 'Jade was scared,' said Shilpa. 'She saw the choppers and said, "I think there's trouble – this is huge." She came out from the Diary Room and she had been crying, and I had an inkling that something was wrong. I saw the fear in her face and I knew it was something big.'

Again and again, though, she urged people, including her fellow countrymen, to be forgiving of Jade. 'When I go back to India, I will make a public appeal for them to forgive her,' she said. 'Asians are overtly sensitive about issues of honour and respect and we will take a stand. I look at the bigger picture. There have been rifts between Asians – this is one time when everybody came together to show their solidarity to their colour. I know the Asians, whether Hindus, Muslims or whatever, will say enough is enough. I am proud of who I am, I have done my bit. The word "racism" should be eradicated from the dictionary; it should have no place in the world. The word doesn't exist for me.'

As for the fact that the trio of girls had been on the receiving end of death threats, Shilpa was appalled. 'That's not the way to deal with this,' she said. 'I would like the police to protect their houses.'

She did, however, say, 'I don't like confrontation but Jade was looking for trouble – you couldn't reason with her. She would just keep talking and didn't seem to listen to anything I said. She was just so noisy. I tried to make myself understood and explain things. But it was like being at the epicentre of an earthquake.' Watching the Oxo saga again, she remarked, 'She's so mean, she's so mean!'

One particular issue that seemed to bring forward an even greater stream of abuse was that Jade thought Shilpa had told her she needed elocution lessons, when in fact what she had really said was 'etiquette'. After that there was no calming Jade down. 'I couldn't understand it,' said Shilpa. 'I said "etiquette". Jade said to me, "I don't understand half the words you use."'

Initially, of course, it had all gone very well. 'I was told that, at any time I felt uncomfortable with something, I didn't have to do it,' said Shilpa. 'I felt very, very safe and I thought I could handle anything. But I had no power over the actions of the other people in the house. When Jade and her mum arrived, it spiralled out of control. The first time I felt discomfort was when Jade started screaming at Dirk about the whisky. I have respect for people older than me and she crossed the line with Dirk.'

Of course, Jackiey's presence only served to make matters worse, especially given her repeated refusal to say Shilpa's name. 'I told her it was like "Ship" with an "l" in the middle but she still wouldn't listen or take it in,' said Shilpa. 'It got annoying. It's only a name and not that difficult. I didn't understand her. I've been a little bit spoiled and pampered but I can get on with anyone. Well, almost anyone ...'

Naturally, there was also massive curiosity about what Shilpa thought of the housemates themselves. Of course, everyone knew who she did and didn't get on with, but so far we hadn't had her actual analysis of their characters. Now, talking to the *Daily Mirror*, she was happy to oblige.

On Jack, she said, 'It was hard to have a conversation because he was very young and attached to Jade. I hated the way he left his dirty underpants in the bathroom. Once I picked them up and had to scrub my hands with antibacterial wash – I nearly took my skin off. He was being mean when he told me to clean out the toilet with my teeth, but I chose to filter that out.' She also refused to watch the footage in which Jack was offensive about her – again, he was using language that must have been anathema to her.

She was fairly complimentary about Donny Tourette, however. 'We had no conversation whatsoever, mainly because we could not understand each other's accents,' she said. 'On the first night, when he jumped into the spa bath with all his clothes on, I was a little scared and thought, "He's trouble – I must stay away from him". But the next day, when he was sober, I realised he was a lovely little mouse and very polite.'

Displaying rather a talent for backhanded compliments, she next turned her attention to Leo. 'Leo talked so much that when he turned mute I enjoyed it,' she said. 'His voice just went on and on so much that I started to lose my focus. I thought he was a real rock and roll star when he left the house the way he did. But, looking back, when he left *Big Brother* the house died because we realised he had been the life and soul. Leo has a good soul and spirit.'

She even managed to be quite nice about Jo. 'She didn't so much as wash her own cup the whole time,' said Shilpa. 'Sometimes she'd be nice, sometimes not. Life has made Jo cynical. Some bad things have happened to her but no one can ever take away her fantastic voice. I'm sad she is unrepentant about the nasty things she said – that means the nice things she said later weren't true. But I never nominated Jo.'

Shilpa and Danielle had, of course, become far friendlier after Jade had gone, to the extent that they almost seemed to form a bond. And though she reiterated the line on Danielle – that she wasn't overburdened in the brains department – the forgiveness shown was wholesale. 'I think Danielle is vulnerable and naive to the point that she sometimes sounds stupid,' she commented. 'I think that because I truly care about her. I worried for her when she had too much to drink because she was trying to salvage her reputation after the Miss Great Britain row but wasn't acting in a ladylike way. I shudder to think about the things she said about going to the loo.'

And then there were the housemates she really got on with, starting with Ian. 'Ian is a darling,' said Shilpa. 'He always really supported me. We had a great bond and I now think of him as a brother. He even straightened my hair on the last night in the house. Ian had his own fears because he had just gone public about being gay. Yet he still steadfastly supported me and I am very, very proud of the way he handled himself during those weeks.'

She also displayed a certain amount of affection for that old rogue Ken Russell. 'I called him "Uncle Ken" because that's a term of affection in India,' said Shilpa. 'He snored a lot, which was my worst fear on *Big Brother*. He stuffed cotton into his nose to stop the noise, and I felt sorry for him. He enjoyed having the servants. He said to Cleo, "That orange is taking a long time, my dear."'

She was rather sweet about Dirk. 'I flirted with Dirk when I needed a distraction, but there was nothing in it, no real chemistry,' she said. 'He is fond of me, but he is a little old for me. I had immense respect for Dirk because he was a big name in television and turned his back on all that to devote his life to his boys.'

Journalist Carole Malone also had gone down well. 'She was the first person I bonded with,' said Shilpa. 'I can't call her a mother figure, because no one can come close to my mum, but it was lovely to have someone wise and her support when my cooking was criticised. I gave her my favourite earrings even though my sister wanted them. My sister will kill me!'

Cleo, too, had been a hit. 'Cleo was wonderful,' said Shilpa. 'When we first met, I thought we probably wouldn't get along because she was so la-di-dah. She has impeccable manners and I was impressed with that.

She was the elegant one in the house, not me. She did lots of housework and became official *BB* dishwasher.'

But there was no doubt as to who was her favourite: Jermaine. 'I love him!' she said, in her interview. 'He is the most wonderful person that ever walked the earth – kindness and calmness personified. He talked the most sense and was a saviour in every situation. He never once said "fart", even though I coaxed him, but "flatulated". He never raised his voice; he taught me so much.'

This only left Jade and her mother: 'She is aggressive and needs to attend anger-management classes,' said Shilpa of the former. 'Definitely. She has been through a lot and that's damaged her. I didn't tell her she needed elocution lessons but etiquette lessons. And she will have learned a lesson. I hope police guard her house and she doesn't come to harm.'

As for Jackiey: 'Jackiey and I clashed right away but I don't know why,' Shilpa admitted. 'She was impossible to talk to, but she clearly wasn't all there – everyone could see that immediately. She annoyed me by not making an effort to say my name. She made me cry so many times. It was harder to deal with her than Jade.'

So there you had it: Shilpa was out, having proved

herself under the most trying of circumstances. It was a long way from what she was used to, and also a very long way from where she started out.

8

She Must Have Been a Beautiful Baby

In retrospect, it was obvious she was going to be a beauty. Shilpa's parents, Surendra and Sunanda, were themselves both models in their youth – Surendra for Year glasses and Sunanda for Forhans, Bournvita. And when Shilpa, the eldest of two daughters, was born on 8 June 1975 in Karnataka, southern India, she was an attractive child right from the start. Four years later her younger sister, Shamita, was born, and the family's happiness was complete.

According to Sunanda, she was aware even before Shilpa was born that she was going to be something special. 'During the third month of my pregnancy I started to show dangerous signs of succumbing to a miscarriage,' she said. 'I bled for 21 days and the doctors advised me to abort, but I felt her will to live. So I took to my bed for a couple of months and things righted themselves. I came close to losing her again during my seventh month, when I tumbled heavily down a flight of concrete stairs. Everyone said it was a miracle that nothing happened. I saw it as a sign that my child would be a great survivor. I almost died. The baby was distressed and I was unconscious for 24 hours. Afterwards, once I had recovered, I just felt that she was here for a reason and that the Lord had a role for her to play on this earth.'

Perhaps because she had felt such a strong connection with her daughter even before she was born, Sunanda and Shilpa have always been extremely close. Indeed, at times Shilpa has said that it seemed as if she was the mummy's girl and her sister Shamita was the daddy's girl. Famously, Sunanda has almost always escorted her daughter everywhere, the exception being, of course, the *Big Brother* household, where for the first time in her life she was forced to go it alone.

Indeed, the full extent of her deprivation, if it could be called that, was far greater than most people at first realised. These days, the Shettys and their two daughters live in a huge flat in Mumbai, which takes up the entire floor of the apartment building in which it is based. Inside, the walls are covered with pictures of Hindu deities, with Ganesha, the elephant god of success, given particular predominance, while animal print cushions and plastic flowers decorate the space.

The family live in the kind of style that is only possible these days in Britain for the unfeasibly rich: servants, two bodyguards and two drivers. After Shilpa had gone into the house, it emerged that a servant brought her breakfast in bed every morning and, because she doesn't like to be seen without make-up, she turns her face away until the servant departs. And, although Shilpa is now a wealthy woman in her own right, this lifestyle is down to her parents, not her. She was brought up in luxury, the much-doted-on elder child of wealthy parents, which explains a great deal about why there was such a huge cultural clash between her and the girls when she entered the *Big Brother* house. Had she, say, been sharing the space with Lord this or the Duke of that, things might have been very different.

The family was a member of the Bunt community, speaking Tulu as their first language, but, like most well-educated girls of her background, Shilpa went on to speak at least another seven, possibly more, languages. When Shilpa was two, Sunanda (who considers herself to be something of an astrologer) again felt that great things awaited her daughter when, as she says, she saw Bollywood in the stars. Back then, however, no one had a clue how successful Shilpa was going to be, ultimately making a name for herself not just in Bollywood, but also the West.

The young Shilpa was a lively child: her mother would sometimes call her a 'fightercock', mainly because of spats with Shamita. But the family was a close one: while Shilpa's nickname to most people was 'Manya', Sunanda would call her 'babucha', or 'honeybunch'. Initially, she went to St Anthony's Girls convent in Chembur and then later to Podar College. An athletic girl, she became baseball captain of the school and became a black belt in karate.

Sita Raman, who was principal of Podar College when Shilpa was a student, has fond memories of her old pupil. 'She was always a bright and popular student,' she recalled. 'Although not particularly academic, she shone in creative, cultural and arts studies. She was also exceptionally skilled at Tae Kwon Do. Shilpa had this aura about her which made some believe that she would become a star, and, sure enough, she got her big break while she was still a student here and left to become an actress. I am not surprised that she has become so popular, she is an extremely nice person.'

While she was still very young, Shilpa decided on the direction in which she wanted her life to go. Unsurprisingly, given her parents' early experiences as models, Shilpa decided that she, too, wanted a career in front of the camera, and at the age of 15 she approached a photographer living opposite the family apartment and asked him to take pictures of her. Her career as a model immediately took off, as she signed up with a leading model agency, although she was thwarted in her ultimate ambition: to become a catwalk model. At 5 feet and 7 inches, she was too short (Shilpa mysteriously grew another three inches as she moved into acting).

Even so, some people were taken aback. Her parents were by now successful business people, running a string of their own companies, and Shilpa had been expected to join the family firm – indeed, she had even started to study commerce with a view to doing just that. Nor had anyone other than her mother realised the potential of her looks. 'It was rather ironic as until then Shilpa, while pretty, had not been thought of as the real beauty in the family,' said a friend of the

Shettys. 'Her sister Shamita had a much fairer complexion and Shilpa used to complain about being darker. Her mother would tell her she was a beauty and she must be patient.' Even then, Sunanda was clearly aware that far greater things lay ahead.

'Mum says I was an ugly duckling who grew into an elegant swan,' said Shilpa. 'I was always the scrawny girl at school – tall and gangly, with skinny legs covered in bruises from volleyball and karate. When I started in films, the Indian papers ripped me apart because I made so many disastrous make-up faux pas. But I've picked up a lot of tips from make-up artists and stylists. I'd rate my looks as 7 out of 10 without make-up – and 9 out of 10 with it.'

But it took years to develop that kind of style. Just as it took her over half a decade to find her feet in Bollywood, so Shilpa started out far from being the glossy star that she is today. But she is nothing if not determined, and so, as she battled her way into Bollywood, she also began to learn how to make the best of herself, with stunning results. Again, however, it should not be a surprise that Shilpa doesn't consider herself to be beautiful. Body image is formed as a child and, if, as a child, Shilpa was accustomed to a more tomboy image, then it is hardly surprising that she doesn't always subscribe to the popular image of herself today.

She has also worked out the secret of allure, as well as taking a fairly stern approach to staying slim. 'I take it as a great compliment when someone calls me sexy, but it doesn't come from flashing lots of flesh,' she says. 'Sex appeal comes from the way you carry yourself. There is nothing wrong with wearing something low-cut, but there's a thin line between sensuality and vulgarity.

'I wear a silver chain around my waist that rides up when I've put on weight – that's when I know I've gone overboard with my favourite puddings. The key to a good body is simple: eat well and exercise. If you are working like a dog and eating like a pig, it won't work. I do get the odd spot. I'm not a conventional beauty, but I work hard on my looks. We should all make time for ourselves without worrying about being vain.'

That rather modest assessment of her looks is actually quite typical of Shilpa and indicative of someone who has learned how to make the best of what she has (admittedly with pretty good material to work with). Nor is this modesty a recent development: she has always been open about the fact that she does not consider herself to be beautiful. 'I have a personality, people tell me that, but I am not conventionally beautiful,' she said, in 1997. 'You don't have to be beautiful to be an actress. It's the presence that is important. You can be the most beautiful person on this earth, but, if the audience doesn't like you, that's it. Fortunately, the audience likes me and finds my screen presence good, so I am still here.'

But her description of herself was not what everyone else saw. The film industry noticed her striking looks, courtesy of her appearance in an advertisement for the soft drink 'Limca' when she was only 16, and so a career on the screen was born. Shilpa's mother immediately realised what tremendous opportunities now lay ahead: she gave up her job as marketing director of one of the family companies and played a close part both in developing Shilpa's career and in keeping her away from the seamier side of the business.

As her career has grown, so has her management prowess: one film producer who has followed Shilpa's progress throughout the years says that Sunanda 'fights like a tiger defending her cubs' when it comes to sorting out contracts. This shouldn't be confused with the pushy stage mother, though: Sunanda has gone along with her daughter's wishes rather than things being the other way around.

Some members of her family, however, were outraged that Shilpa was going into the film world, with one grandmother not speaking to her for three years on the grounds that, 'Acting was not something that well-brought-up girls did.' And ironically, although that is the sort of view that was widely held in Britain in the Victorian era and not now, in many ways Shilpa resembles a British girl brought up back then. Her clothing is undoubtedly a lot more revealing than that of a Victorian maiden, but her attitudes are not dissimilar – respect your parents, dignity at all times, behave with caution in your dealings with men. Not for her the vulgarity of the modern British young woman: Shilpa in some ways harks back to a time when Britain was a more civilised place than it is today.

But it wasn't just grandparental disapproval she had to contend with, her father wasn't particularly pleased. 'My father was aghast – a Shetty girl joining films – unthinkable,' said Shilpa. 'Today he's known as Shilpa Shetty's father and he's very proud of it.'

Even so, there were a few bumps at the start of her film career, which began when she was only in her teens. Despite her inexperience, she was offered a lead role in the film *Gaata Rahe Mera Dil*, with the actor Rahul Roy playing the male lead. It did not go according to plan. The film was never completed and what seemed initially like a promising career appeared to be over before it had begun. Shilpa, though, proved herself to be made of stern stuff and was not put off by the experience. Just a year later, in 1993, she was offered the role as the victim of a psychopathic boyfriend in the thriller *Baazigar* opposite Shahrukh Khan and Kajol. It was a resounding success and earned her a Filmfare nomination for Best Newcomer, the first of many award nominations.

And so began what was actually to be a very slow rise to fame. Looking at Shilpa today, it would be easy to think that she simply walked into a big career, but nothing could be further from the truth. In fact, there were years of fits and starts before she began to make a real name for herself, years in which she was frequently written off and equally said never to have achieved her full potential. The temptation to pack it in and settle down with a nice man must have been overwhelming at times, and yet still she battled on. They say it is not the way that you react to success that defines you but how you handle failure, and Shilpa proved, time and again, that she was a fighter who was determined to win through.

This was all the more impressive given that she had

never really planned to be an actress – it had come about almost by chance. Shilpa herself realised that her career was almost as an accident, but, once offered the opportunity, she seized it with both hands. 'It's by chance that I was modelling and I got this offer,' she said in an interview some years ago. 'I accepted it and I loved it. I was warned that this profession was not a nice one to be in, but believe me, that's not true at all – it's just the way you are.

'You are good or bad here or in any other profession. Frankly, I wasn't serious about my career during *Baazigar*. But afterwards, I liked it when people recognised me and mobbed me on the roads, saw a photograph in the magazine. I hate the yellow [unethical, scandal-mongering] journalism that goes with it, though. So it sort of grew on me and now I am very serious about acting.'

She had to be, for Shilpa was born with a determined streak and now it would be put to the test as never before. After *Baazigar*, a successful future seemed assured, and yet she promptly went on to appear in a string of flops, with some people feeling that she had made the wrong decisions about which films to take on because she was still extremely young. At any rate, whatever the reason, she was about to discover that a good debut does not necessarily ease the path ahead.

Shilpa's second film was called *Aag*, a movie she made with the actor Govinda, and which was also notable for the debut of another famous Indian actress, Sonali Bendre. Govinda was very impressed with his beautiful colleague, but the public was not: the film was not a success. There followed in short succession films that included *Hathkadi*, *Chote Sarkar*, *Gambler* and *Pardesi Babu* – Bollywood churns out movies at a rate that makes the inhabitants of Tinseltown seem like slackers – but, again, none seemed to live up to her early promise. There were plenty of people willing to label her just a pretty girl: even now, her body and her ability to dance are spoken of as much as her range in her acting career, and that despite the fact that some of her later roles were to be far more serious than anything she did at the start. And her dancing certainly didn't hold her back. As she herself has said on many occasions, it's her unique selling point – other Indian actresses might look as good as her and act even better, but very few can dance anything like as well.

Not that it seemed to make much difference back then. Shilpa had fans within the industry and an enormous amount of drive, however, which is how, well over a decade after these early failures, she was able to kick-start a whole new career in the West. Back then, such a possibility was remote, though. Everything possible was done to help her on her way: she was offered roles with some major stars in order to get her noticed – her leads included Sunny Deol in *Himmat* and Saif Ali Khan in *Aao Pyar Karen* – yet still there was no major breakthrough. It began to look as if her early success was a fluke. Her younger sister Shamita also became an actress and in some ways overtook Shilpa, but anyone who thought she was prepared to give up was in for a big surprise.

For a start, she might not have been Bollywood's most successful actress but all this work did have its financial rewards, and she was becoming wealthy in her own right. Estimates vary wildly as to what she got paid: figures of £500,000 per film have been bandied around recently, although it is unlikely she was getting anything near that then. But she was being well rewarded and her parents were looking after her growing fortune carefully, with the result that she may now be worth up to £15 million.

To further her financial endeavours, she did some largely forgettable films in the southern part of India, which didn't do much for her status as an actress, but did pay well. She was especially keen on one role, that of a mermaid in a movie called *Saagar Kanya*, but, again, the film failed to do any significant business.

Then, in 1994, the people who helped her to initial success decided to take a hand. The company behind *Baazigar* was an outfit called Venus, run by the Jain brothers. They still had faith in their new discovery and cast her in a film called *Main Khiladi Tu Anari*, with Khiladi Akshay Kumar. Things finally appeared to look up when the film was a great success and one of its numbers – 'Chura ke dil mera goriya chali' – became a hit on its own, going on to become one of the most popular songs of the year.

While Shilpa would have been forgiven for thinking her worries were over, she was wrong. Despite the success of the film, her career inexplicably continued to stall. She didn't seem able to make the breakthrough towards becoming one of the major stars of the day, but there was no particular reason why. Shilpa is a perfectly good actress (her comparison of herself to Angelina Jolie is probably correct in terms of acting ability, if not status) and yet still she struggled to be taken seriously. Her height – she was now, at 5'10, one of the tallest of the Bollywood actresses – seemed to excite as much comment as anything else. On the screen, however, she just couldn't make that final, significant break.

Her next film, from which much was expected, was called *Laal Badshah*. It was widely thought that she wanted to do it because the lead was a very famous actor called Amitabh Bachchan, while the director was KC Bokadia. Indeed, so keen was she to do the film that it was rumoured Shilpa had even forgone payment for the role. It was no good, however; still she didn't manage that much-longed-for breakthrough.

With each film that failed to take off, Shilpa's determination seemed to grow. She enjoyed the limelight, as she admitted herself, and, if it came to that, she enjoyed the filmmaking process, too. And no one could deny that she looked pretty good in what she did, was professional, turned up on time, did her work and didn't make a fuss. Though Shilpa might have some diva-ish qualities, she certainly wasn't going to allow them to get in the way of her ambitions. Yet, for totally inexplicable reasons, her metamorphosis from starlet to serious actress just would not come.

Given that her determination remained as strong as ever, and that by this time she had had not only a good few years in the business but also a whole host of flops to her name, Shilpa's resilience in the *Big Brother* household can be put into context: the odd screaming match with Jade is nothing compared to years of hard work and disappointment. And yet, to her enormous credit, she soldiered on.

Indeed, she showed what lengths she was prepared to go to by having a nose job on the recommendation of one of her directors, Dharmesh Darshan, and was totally up front about it, too. Questioned about the change in her appearance, Shilpa showed a degree of honesty lacking in your average Hollywood actress: 'A nose job in today's time is as common as threading – come on,' she said.

Her honesty was commendable, but still her acting career failed to take off.

Indeed, by this time, without meaning to sound catty, her real talent appeared to be in choosing dud films. Next up was a lead in *Dhadkan*, again courtesy of Venus, directed by Dharmesh Darshan, and starring Sunil Shetty and Akshay Kumar; it promptly ran into problems when Sunil Shetty was replaced by Arbaaz Khan, who in turn was replaced by Sunil Shetty again. Whether or not he was fed up with the shenanigans, Darshan shelved the project temporarily and went off to make another film, *Mela*, instead. At the time, it seemed that *Dhadkan* was not going to be another failure, but that it wouldn't even get made in the first place. In the event, things were finally about to come good for Shilpa.

Whatever her feelings about what had happened to *Dhadkan* and the state of her career at the time, she had a great deal more to occupy her, for she had by now embarked on her first serious relationship: with her co-star Akshay Kumar. Though this was her deepest relationship to date, whatever happiness she might have been feeling in her personal life did not spill over into the professional arena: her career resolutely refused to budge.

By this time, Shilpa had been making movies for about six years and she could well and truly have been forgiven for giving up, but instead she made two films in quick succession – *Shool* and *Tarkeib* – only to be excused of vulgarity in song and dance sequences such as 'Main Aayi hoon U.P. Bihar Lootne' in *Shool*. Again, Shilpa would not allow herself to be discouraged. 'In fact, people thought I was the saving grace in both the films,' she said, effectively silencing her critics.

Her appearance in *Shool* was not a lengthy one, but, despite the carping, it finally heralded a change in her fortunes. Indeed, you could say the film rescued her. Far from finding her dancing vulgar, audiences loved it, giving a very much-needed new lease of life to her career. But even that had its downside and Shilpa herself was lately prone to complaining that people noticed her body rather than her acting abilities, although, compared to being ignored, it was no bad fate. 'I did just one number in *Shool*. That, too, because I needed to get noticed then. But people are making it out as if I made a career out of dance numbers. From now on, all my *jhatka-matkas* [a popular form of Bollywood dancing involving lots of gyrations] will be reserved for my regular flicks. No more guest appearances for me.'

As the years passed, Shilpa, while still not making any great headway, had learned a good deal. For a start, there was her appearance: always groomed and polished to the nth degree, she certainly looked the part of a huge movie star, even if she wasn't quite that yet. She took her appearance seriously – there were rumours of further nose jobs – while she worked out methodically to stay ahead of the pack.

9
Shilpa Makes the Grade

It had been years in coming but finally, in 2000, Shilpa made the breakthrough. Dharmesh Darshan made a movie called *Mela* (coincidentally starring Twinkle Khanna, the woman Akshay would leave Shilpa for), but it was a flop. In need of a film to restore his reputation, he returned to *Dhadkan*, some years after he had shelved it, and brought his original stars back on board. By this time Shilpa and Akshay (whom she had met on the set of *Dhadkan*) had split up but, resolutely professional, neither of them told anyone else and they got on with making the film. If it was a struggle to act with her old boyfriend, it was one that paid off for Shilpa. The film was a hit, she was taken seriously and for the first time in her life she began to get the sort of recognition she had always craved.

Of course, there had been some fine tuning of the film script in the intervening years, but Shilpa was not concerned. 'Changes always happen and they're usually for the betterment of the film,' she said. 'Dharmeshji as the director was the captain of the ship. He knew what was best for his ship. I believed in him and just sailed along. It was not my job to worry about what he was doing. And why would I need to be worried? My role hasn't changed; the basic storyline is the same. Dharmeshji has only made some modifications to add to the screenplay and enhance the look of the film.'

The film was a slightly unusual one considering its audience, as Shilpa herself explained. 'Usually, in a Hindi film, the heroine isn't supposed to get involved in a relationship before marriage and, if she does, it's usually treated as a dark secret and never alluded to directly,' she said. 'What's nice about Hindi films is that they are always trying to uphold Indian values and tradition, but what's even nicer is when a film like *Dhadkan* comes along, and has no qualms in projecting a heroine who had loved a man and married another. Anjali [her character] has a past. She accepts it and carries on with her life. You can't live on love and fresh air, you know. Also, she loves her parents and does what they think is best for her.'

What made all this particularly enticing to the starstruck audience of India was that it was well known that Shilpa and Akshay were in a relationship (although the break-up was not yet public). Could she, the audience delighted in speculating, be talking about her own experiences?

Certainly Shilpa was aware that was one view people might take. 'What's beautiful about *Dhadkan* is that the story's so real it could happen to any of us,' she continued. 'There must be so many women in our country who have gone through what Anjali does in the film. Sometime in your life, you must have had a crush on someone. But maybe he didn't fit into your scheme of things, and you went ahead and made your life with someone else. Even the thought is giving me gooseflesh. But, because Anjali's situation is so unfilmy, it is easy to identify and empathise with her.'

Her personal life aside, though, Shilpa herself was ecstatic with her new role, and it shone through. At long last, she was beginning to be regarded as more than a brilliant dancer with the best body in

Bollywood: people were finally starting to take her seriously. 'As for my career, I have been getting roles with a lot of scope to perform,' she said in an interview after the film was released. 'There is a lot of variety in the roles I'm doing now.

'I am also getting a lot of positive feedback, which is a good feeling. That is something I have been working on for a very long time. I have been in the film industry for seven years. And I'm only now getting what I should have had a long time ago. It feels good. Better late than never, I say! But I can tell you one thing: every film of mine from now on will get me praise as an actress. I am very positive about that. You see, the films I am now choosing are very different from the ones I used to earlier.'

For anyone who thinks this sounds a little overconfident, it should be remembered that Shilpa comes from a very different culture to the West and what sounds OTT is not necessarily seen the same way there. And she could clearly hardly contain herself. Success had been a long, long time in coming; she was going to enjoy it now it was there. She was also aware that many of her early choices had not been ideal and was prepared to learn from her mistakes. At long last, having got the career she had hoped for for so long, it was now more a question of taking full advantage of the opportunities open to her.

Sometimes she could also sound a little bit defensive. Asked if the film was a 'major change' for her, she replied, 'You're making it sound as if this was the first time I was performing. I've performed in my other films too, haven't I? What made *Dhadkan* different is that this isn't a run-of-the-mill commercial film, where the story revolves entirely around the hero and his doings. This is a film about relationships and every character has a significant role to play in carrying the story forward. Perhaps that's the reason every member of the cast has come up with a performance that's sure to stand out. No doubt, *Dhadkan* is a very special film for me. I was lucky to get the opportunity to work with a talented director like Dharmesh Darshan. I grabbed it and made the best of it.'

This is almost exactly what she had said about her entry into the film business: it was clearly Shilpa's philosophy to grab opportunities when they were available and run with it. It was what she was to do in the *Big Brother* house seven years hence.

She was also very aware that this was the chance to prove herself to be a serious actress rather than just a pretty face. 'Well, I do have this image of being very glamorous and that has sometimes overpowered the performer in me,' she said. 'Dharmeshji did not make a conscious effort to make me look less glamorous, but, yes, he did work hard on portraying me as an actress, rather than a glamorous star. I know this is kind of confusing, but I really can't explain it better. The heroine of *Dhadkan* is a stylish, modern miss, who's beautiful in every which way. She's glamorous, too, but, to use one of my oft-repeated phrases, the role is not just about lashes and lipstick. This film is not about Shilpa Shetty, it's about Anjali and there's more to her than just a pretty face. She's the kind of person you'd want to know better.'

Indeed, if anything, she was relieved that in this particular film someone else had done the glamour act and she was also pleased that the role didn't involve dancing. 'For the first time I have not been projected as a girl who dances well,' she said. 'All the songs have been picturised on me, but for once I'm not doing any dancing. It's Mahima's turn this time and it was a welcome change for me to watch another heroine dance.'

Quite what an about-turn this represented in her career was illustrated by the fact that she was nominated for an award for her performance: Best

Actress in the International Indian Film Awards. Shilpa
had been up for the odd award in the past – indeed,
she'd won Best Supporting Actress in 1998 for *Pardesi
Babu* in the Zee Gold Bollywood Awards – but this was
different. For the first time, it was her work that was
the focal point, while she was also being talked about
now with genuine respect. It had been a long time
coming, but a combination of optimism,
determination, talent and self-confidence had finally
taken her where she wanted to go. This certainly didn't
guarantee it would all be plain sailing from now on – it
wasn't – but it marked a real advance in a career that
had taken a while to get going.

Of course, Shilpa was still living at home with her
parents and at around this time she had her one and
only thought of rebellion. 'My sister and I are never
allowed to lock our doors and Dad has CCTV
cameras in the hall, kitchen and dining areas,' she told
the *Mirror*. 'His favourite hobby is watching them. I
don't drink and always have to be in for 2am, so now
and then I plead with Dad and say, "But the party
doesn't even start until 11pm!" That sometimes
softens him up.

'Once, when I was 27, I tried to rebel. I said to Dad,
"I've been earning my own money, a lot of money, for

years now. If I want to stay out until after 2am, I will!"
He handed me a big bundle of bank papers and said,
"Fine. If you want to look after yourself, find another
house and take care of all these." I shuddered. I have
no head for figures and don't even know how much I
earn. And I love living with my parents. I turned into a
little mouse and said, "OK, I'll be home by 2am."
People might think living by all my parents' rules is odd
at 31, but that's just the way we live in India, and I love
that about my country.'

Certainly, it is almost inconceivable that a
Hollywood star of Shilpa's standing would still be
living with her parents and allowing them to tell her
what to do, but it has stood her in remarkably good
stead. For a start, it gave her a degree of emotional
protection that many of her Western counterparts have
notably lacked, which in turn provided her with a
stable base from which to pursue her career. To an
extent, it also protected her from becoming involved in
scandal. Although Shilpa and Akshay were known to
be an item, there would never have been the slightest
question of them living together. There was a sense of
propriety about the relationship that is almost
inconceivable in the West today and which, if truth be
told, only added to Shilpa's appeal.

In this new phase of her life and career, she was very open about her own mistakes, talking about them in relation to Shamita, who had just started out on her own film career. 'Well, she is a smart girl. I was the foolish one; I came from a non-film background,' she said. 'I learned everything on my own. She has seen me go through all that. We have told her only one thing, "You don't need to sign any films because you want to buy a car or a house." We have all that. It's not that I signed films because of that; it's just that in the beginning you don't know – you don't have anyone to give you the right advice. Shamita can learn from my mistakes. That's the reason she is not on a signing spree. Films are coming her way but she'd rather work on maybe two or three films a year and find job satisfaction as an artiste. That is essential. I think job satisfaction is the key word.'

The fact that Shamita now was also an actress meant that Shilpa's mother had to look after both girls. Initially, Shilpa found it a bit hard. 'You know, while I was shooting for *Dhadkan*, my mother had accompanied Shamita to London for the shooting of *Mohabbatein*,' she said. 'It was so strange. For the first five days, I just kept crying at home. It was very depressing. You know, she has always been Daddy's girl, and I've always spent time with Mum. But, for the first time, I realised how much my sister must have sacrificed for me. At her most vulnerable age, Mum was with me, and she never complained. That is when I began to appreciate all that she has done for me.'

After the success of *Dhadkan*, Shilpa's star continued to rise, although initially, and unsurprisingly, given past setbacks, she thought it was a one-off. 'After *Dhadkan*, I felt it was my dream role,' she said. 'But now, there are a few interesting roles like in Salman's film. I thought after *Dhadkan* I would never get a role like that again. A heroine-oriented role, I thought, would be very difficult to get. But people are offering me such amazing roles that I feel like a new heroine. It's really great. I feel I have rediscovered myself after *Dhadkan*.'

And the very fact that she'd been around for such a long time in some ways worked in her favour. Shilpa does not lack self-belief, but even she admitted to down periods when she thought she was getting nowhere, and now she could hardly believe her luck. 'I think my strength is that, even after seven years, people see a different Shilpa with every film,' she said philosophically. 'That is something I have maintained all throughout. And people still want to work with me after being here so long. Recently, I went through a very low phase – there was so much I wanted to do, but just didn't get the right chance. Today I am happy I'm getting that opportunity to do so. And I'm quite content. As for my weaknesses, I'm working on turning them around so that they become my forte.'

She continued to make films at a rate of knots, but these were much better regarded than her older films and she was given a lot of praise. Among the work she was doing was *Indian*, which went on to become another highly acclaimed role, directed by Maharajan. 'In *Indian*, I play Sunny Deol's wife, a very emotional girl who loves her father very much,' said Shilpa. 'The film has a lot of action, but it is a family film, too. What appealed to me was that this girl's character is very well etched. She has two children, is very homely and her world revolves around her husband.'

But that was not all, not by a long shot. There was also a Bobby Kent film with Salman Khan, and a Satish Kaushik and Anil Kapoor Entertainment film – *Badhai Ho Badhai* – starring opposite Anil Kapoor and directed by Satish Kaushik. In addition, in *Junoon*, Shilpa was paired with Chandrachur Singh, and there was a film directed by Yashji Chopra's assistant, *Abhi*. It was quite a workload.

Shilpa was extremely keen to talk about her new

roles. 'In Bobby Kent's film, I play a very young and vulnerable model,' she said. 'She is very modern and falls in love with someone she thinks is very modern but only poses to be one before marriage. He comes from a very orthodox family with very Indian values, whereas in my house it is just the opposite. We are very Western and we think we've come from London! So it is a clash of two cultures and how things change after marriage. I think it is a beautiful subject. It is a very real film and something I would relate to.'

The filming, however, was not without incident. Shilpa was almost quite badly hurt in the middle of it all, although she herself played the episode down. 'We were shooting a *suhag raat* [a typical Bollywood honeymoon] scene and there were lights on the bed,' she said. 'I didn't realise that. We were supposed to go out of frame. That is when I fell on the lights and got burned. It was only the next day that I realised that it was bad and I had to get it treated. I still have the marks on my body.

'But it was nothing serious, and I certainly don't think Salman should be blamed for that. Salman is like a great buddy of mine. He is the kind of friend I have had for the last six years. I have done many shows with him. I have worked with him and his brother Sohail before in *Auzaar*. I have worked with Arbaaz in *Dhadkan* before Sunil came in for the role. Salman is not a fairweather friend and is the kind of person I can totally rely on.'

She was also very enthusiastic about the other films in the pipeline. 'Satishji's film has me playing a very vivacious and loud Punjabi girl,' she said. 'That again is something I haven't done before. Her character is a mix between a Punjabi and a Christian, and her name is Banto Betty. [*Junoon*] is very interesting. I play an intelligent and spunky youngster, who's the brain behind her father's political career. He is a minister. She is very bold, open and honest about her feelings. She is very cool and a very today kind of girl; doesn't care what the world thinks about her. At the same time she's a very passionate person.'

Nor was that all she was doing. Shilpa's work was not just confined to film: she did shows, too, in which her dancing and singing were put to good use. 'Yeah, I am doing a lot of shows,' she said, at the time. 'I have some good songs right now and I should cash in on that, right? Also, I'm a workaholic and I can't sit at home twiddling my thumbs. If I get a good show and the money's great, I go ahead and do it. I prefer doing a good show to doing a bad film.'

Of course, by this stage in her career, whatever she might have felt about the attention paid to her appearance as well as her acting, Shilpa had become a bona fide style icon, looked up to and emulated by millions of Bollywood fans. As such, she was asked a lot about the secrets behind her style. 'According to me, like many others, "beauty lies in the eyes of the beholder,"' she said. 'Even today if someone tells me they find me beautiful, I get surprised. Honestly, I don't think I am because I know I'm not conventionally beautiful. And, even if I was to presume I were, what's my contribution to it? It's God's grace that has made me the way I am and the genes I've inherited from my beautiful parents.'

Unlike her Hollywood counterparts, Shilpa said she did not feel the need to look constantly beautiful. 'No, I've never looked at it from this perspective,' she said. 'Since we actors are considered trendsetters, whatever we wear starts an entire style of clothing. Like say, torn jeans! I may wear it due to some personal constraints, but it becomes a style statement with the youth. But that's not pressurising because I'm not dressing in a particular way to please people. Talking about myself, I never alter my styles depending on what's trendy now. Even today I have no issue about wearing a decade-old pair of jeans. But what's important is that it has to suit my image and make me feel comfortable.'

And she was pretty good humoured about it all. Asked when she first became aware of fashion, she replied, 'I remember in college, once I'd gone all decked up, wearing a lovely yellow polo neck T-shirt and black trousers. On entering the premises, I overheard guys calling me "taxi". That's when I first got fashion conscious. After this particular incident, I started reading a lot about fashion, trends, styles and the like.

'When I'm not shooting, you'll find me casually clad in a loose T-shirt with pajamas or a simple casual dress. In Western casuals, I like a good pair of jeans or a short skirt coupled with a tight-fitting top, or a long, good-fit slit gown, along with matching accessories like the same-coloured belt, shoes and bag/purse to go with it. Of course, if it's a special occasion or event, then I prefer formal wear. A beautiful sari or *salwar-kameez* [a typical dress throughout South Asia, comprising loose trousers and a long tunic top] adorned with the necessary jewellery would be my perfect choice. I think the sari is the most sensual wear.'

Of course, she had picked up many of the tricks of the trade as she'd gone along, and now knew how to make the best of herself. 'Over the years, my sense of make-up has changed considerably,' she said. 'Initially I'd think, if I apply more make-up, I'd look more beautiful. Hence I'd apply more eye shadow, gloss and darker shades of lipstick. But now my perception has changed completely. The "no-make-up look" suits me the best. Let me add here that I'm extremely fond of lipstick. My folks tease me that I'd even wear a shade to the bathroom. Mac beauty products is my favourite international brand, and in Indian brands, it's Lux.'

Her professional routine was, however, different. 'Of course, when shooting, pancake is used, which is very different from the normal make-up routine,' she said. 'If the shooting hours are very long, then I put on pancake twice. After a considerable time of shooting when we get a long break, I remove the greasepaint and reapply fresh pancake. Also, if I can catch up with some sleep, I do so, because it makes me feel fresh. Like my mother, I too never apply soap to my face. I use a face wash. In between shots, I drink lots of water. After pack-up, I take almost half an hour to remove the greasepaint. And, no matter how tired I am, I never sleep with my make-up on.'

Shilpa also paid a great deal of attention to her hair. 'When I'm not shooting, I get oil massages done,' she said. 'And after two hours, I wash it with a good conditioner. Even in my busiest schedules, I religiously condition my hair. It's a misconception that your hair grows if you apply a lot of oil. An extensive use of it will not result in longer, thicker hair.'

When in the *Big Brother* house, Shilpa had entranced the nation with her fantastic collection of earrings: this, too, was a passion that went back a long way. 'I like the ancient ethnic Indian jewellery,' she said. 'They remain in style no matter what the current trend is. I also like both uncut as well as polished diamonds and am fond of stones. But I have an aversion to heavy, glossy gold jewellery. Gold with a matt finish entices me the most. I've worn a lot of silver jewellery – I'm bored of it now.'

And her beauty tip? 'Outer beauty is peripheral,' said Shilpa. 'I believe that it's inner beauty that's most important. More than being called sexy, beautiful, glamorous, I would want to be remembered as a good human being. That's my take on beauty.'

It was all good advice, which has clearly stood her in very good stead. You don't maintain a reputation for having the best body in Bollywood in the face of some very stiff competition without serious hard work. Shilpa had learned an enormous amount in her time in the business, in terms of how to stay looking good, as well as about acting. And with this new phase in her career, interest in her was at fever pitch. But, behind the public success, what of her personal life?

The truth is that Shilpa had not had an entirely trouble-free time there, either. At the time of writing, she is still single at 31, which, as she herself admits, is considered to be quite old in the society in which she lives. Of course, a great many men are enormously attracted to her, both in India and in the West, and it is extremely unlikely that she will maintain this single status. But her love life has not gone smoothly to date, not smoothly at all ...

10
Love Hurts

Like most Indian women of her class and generation, Shilpa is sure that ultimately she will get married, and that there is a strong chance it would be an arranged marriage. Love, she said on *Big Brother*, is an overrated emotion: an arranged marriage has quite as good a chance of working as a love match, and she is almost certainly right. But then Shilpa knew what she was talking about, for, in her mid-twenties, she did have quite a serious love affair, one which she almost certainly hoped would lead to marriage.

But a love match was not out of the question, either. Talking about her film *Dhadkan*, she said, 'I don't think my parents would ever oppose me if I really believed in and loved someone intensely. But, if they did, then they have the right to do so. Our parents are more experienced in the ways of the world; they see things in a wider perspective and would know what's best for us. For me, my parents are God. I would definitely do what they wished, because I know for sure my mum and dad would never do anything to hurt me.'

Unlike – she could but didn't add – her co-star in *Dhadkan*: Akshay Kumar. Akshay (real name Rajiv Hari Om Bhatia) is a very handsome and successful Bollywood actor, who had studied martial arts in Hong Kong before becoming an actor. Seven years Shilpa's senior, he had previously been linked to his co-stars; just before he met Shilpa, he had split up with an actress called Raveena Tandon. Like Shilpa after her, Raveena afterwards said that her relationship with Akshay had held back her career; certainly both romances were to become the subject of intense media scrutiny.

Shilpa, obviously, was aware of what had happened with Raveena and, according to some reports, was also aware that Akshay had never acknowledged the relationship in print. Worried that she, too, might remain in the background, she successfully encouraged him to be more open about it, something which, alas, did nothing to keep the two together in the longer term.

Shilpa, however, was now in a slightly tricky position. On the one hand, she very understandably wanted to be seen as part of a couple; on the other, it was felt she was more marketable as a star if she was regarded as single and available. Indeed, she brought this up on *Big Brother*: while never mentioning Akshay by name, she revealed it had caused problems in her career when she was known to have a boyfriend. At the time, she also successfully sued *Stardust India* for publishing a piece about the relationship.

Then there was the matter of quite how far the relationship progressed. Again, *Big Brother* broadcast a rather uncomfortable scene: Jade demanded to know whether Shilpa had lost her virginity to Akshay. Shilpa, clearly appalled and uncomfortable at the line of questioning, changed the subject as soon as she could.

But she had plainly lost her heart. This was her first big romance, to an older and glamorous man. But the relationship was not to last. At some point, Akshay decided his future lay elsewhere and he began to see the actress Twinkle Khanna, whom he later married and with whom he was to have a son.

Initially, Shilpa remained discreet about what had happened. But, as the split became public and details of Akshay's new relationship emerged, for one of the very few times in her life, she lashed out. And in some ways it was admirable: she felt she had been treated badly and did not hesitate to say so. 'Yes, it has been a rough period personally,' she said, when questioned about the split. 'But I'm glad that the ordeal is over. After every dark cloud, there's always a silver lining. All this while, though things were going well professionally, my personal life was pulling me down. It feels good that it's finally behind me.'

When it was put to her that she was very upset about the break-up, Shilpa responded with a passion her audience had only seen on screen before. 'Don't I have reasons to be upset?' she asked. 'When you love someone and all along don't realise that you are being taken for a ride, it can be very annoying. I never imagined that he could two-time me, and that too all along our relationship.'

Asked why she was speaking out now, she replied, 'I wanted our film to get over and released, so that it wouldn't come in the way of my producers. I couldn't harass them just because my personal life was turning into shambles. So, I decided to wait till *Dhadkan* was done with.' And, when it was put to her that Akshay said she shouldn't make a big issue about it, she continued, 'That's his opinion, not mine. After what he did with me, what else could he say? See, I don't regret my decision at all. Someone has to let people know about him and warn all the other women to keep off him. Besides, I was very angry and wanted to let him know that he could not get away with murder.'

Was she upset with Twinkle? 'No, I'm not at all upset with her,' said Shilpa. 'What's her fault if my man was cheating on me? There is no point blaming any other woman, it was entirely his fault. Akshay Kumar used me and conveniently dropped me after he found someone else. The only person I was upset with was him, but I'm sure he'll get it all back.

'It's not easy to forget the past so soon, but I'm glad I've had the strength to move on. Today, he's a forgotten chapter as far as I'm concerned. I will never work with him again. Professionally, things have never looked better – I've signed five new films. So, I confidently say that I've moved on after our split.'

But those words didn't sound like those of someone who'd moved on and Shilpa was, indeed, badly hurt. Despite plenty of male attention, she was in no hurry to rush into another relationship. Akshay, meanwhile, was adamant he had not promised to commit to her. 'I had only told her that let's see how this relationship works out then decide to go steady,' he said.

But Shilpa was determined this experience wouldn't turn her off men. 'I'm not scared of falling in love, nor have I become cynical about love after my experience with Akshay,' she said some months later. '*Pyaar ho jaata hai, kiya nahin jaata* [Love happens, one doesn't decide to do it]. Right now, my career is very important; it's like I have to hit the bull's-eye in my career and I can't see myself getting married for a really long time, at least not till I achieve my goals.'

Time, though, does seem to have healed that particular wound. At the end of 2006, Akshay was quoted as saying that, if he bumped into Shilpa, he'd say a polite hello and move on. Shilpa's response was spirited. 'Why should it just be a polite hello?' she said. 'It would be a hearty hello from my side! I have nothing against Akshay Kumar – we have done quite a few shows together. There is no ill-feeling from my side. Life's too short to hold any grudges.' That episode, at least, was clearly in the past.

A relationship with the musician and composer Sandeep Chowta followed, although, despite marriage rumours, that was also not to last. Rumours, hotly denied by everyone said to be involved, began to circulate that Shilpa had become close to a married man, or, to be more precise, film director Anubhav

Sinha. He had directed Shilpa on the film *Dus*, which was filmed in Canada, and shortly afterwards had split with his wife Ratna. He himself was adamant no one else was involved. 'It has nothing to do with Shilpa Shetty, but I don't really want to talk about the reasons that we have separated.'

Friends, as so often in these cases, were eager to say their bit. 'Anubhav and Ratna have always had compatibility problems. They tried to sort out their issues by separating for a while,' said one, adding that the split had now become permanent. 'The problem is not other people, but the couple themselves. They've tried to work it out. Living separately was a solution but even that didn't help.'

Shilpa's sister was cast in one of his next films, *Cash*. And Bollywood longed for a romance between Anubhav and Shilpa. 'Please!' said Anubhav, when asked the question directly. 'Are you mad? Shilpa is a wonderful friend and that's all there is to this rumour.'

Yet still the rumours wouldn't go away. As recently as November 2006, Bollywood fantasised that there would be a wedding the following year to which Anubhav again responded by laughing it off. 'What date and venue? Does she know about it? Ha, ha, ha, ha! *Arre kaam karne de yaar* [Let me work, pal],' he said.

Shilpa herself had no desire to comment, although she did offer this view about modern marriage. 'Nowadays, women are at par with men,' she said. 'They are educated and their views regarding life have changed. I don't think it is wrong to be confident – I think that is why marriages are breaking these days in our country.'

Never shy about being contrary, the Bollywood rumour machine then began to put out simultaneous opposing stories that Shilpa was seeing politician Milind Deora. She decided to tackle the stories head on. 'I am neither dating Anubhav Sinha nor going around with Milind Deora,' she snapped. 'They are my friends, like many others in the film industry, but unfortunately my friendly relations are misconstrued as love affairs. I am surprised why people are interested in associating my name to persons who I don't even know. This is a deliberate attempt to tarnish my image and my relationships.'

But why, Shilpa was asked, was it happening to her? 'Since I am single, they think that I am ready to mingle,' she said, utilising a phrase that she was to use again, to very good effect, after *Big Brother*. 'But, believe me, it's a curse to be single in this industry. Even if I meet somebody for professional or other social reasons, it is misconstrued. Whether that person is a senior or respectable person in the industry, rumour-mongers really do not care all about this.'

She was also irritated when it was pointed out that she was seen around with many good-looking men in the industry. 'Let me make one thing very clear: that I don't hunt for good-looking men, in and out of the industry. It is rather very unfortunate that people get such impressions because they read about them in print,' she said. 'It's strange that negative things always make good headlines and the positive ones fail to find their way in print and are not highlighted prominently. It's better to refrain from interviews – press tends to customise things as per its requirements.'

But that was far from being her last word on the subject and it does not take a great leap of the imagination to work out why Shilpa was so worked up: a Bollywood star is in the interesting position of having to appear simultaneously desirable and chaste, not always the easiest role to pull off. Nor does she want to be linked to too many men, or that, too, might cause complications. And Shilpa must have felt it very unfair: after all this time working on her career, now her love life was the one thing everyone wanted to know about. 'Last year, my name was linked with three different guys,' she told one journalist. 'Have a heart! I'm neither crazy, nor a man-eater.'

On Anubhav Sinha: 'That's rubbish! Anubhav, as they say, is a good friend. Why should anyone have a problem with that?'

And on Milind Deora: 'Why, why, why?' protested Shilpa. 'Why drag his name in again? The day I find my soul mate, I'll announce it to the world.'

She was then asked if there was any other film star who had a body quite like hers. 'Hello ... that's quite a left-handed compliment,' she responded. 'But I would like to believe there's more to me than my figure. In the movies, it's very difficult to live on looks alone. One has to be talented to make a mark in such a competitive environment. Period. There has been a paradigm shift in the roles that I've portrayed recently. I've become an actress who can look good and emote as well. I know I'm being immodest, but isn't honesty a bigger virtue than modesty?'

Shilpa's performance in the *Big Brother* household means she has now widened her potential circle of admirers worldwide. Since her emergence from the house, the West has been quite fascinated to hear not just about her past life, but also about the way her relationships, as a modern Indian woman, are handled.

The answer is: very differently from those in the West.

Talking to the *Mirror*, she explained the rites of Indian courtship. 'I'm single and ready to mingle!' she said, using what is clearly a favourite phrase. '[But] if a guy wants to take me out, he must seek my dad's permission first – that's just the way it works. I secretly brief them about the best answers to give to my father's questions before they face him. But that hasn't stopped Dad vetoing a good few. I try not to mind when that happens because parents are always right in the long run.'

And even men who make the grade are not allowed an easy life. 'Even when Mum and Dad give me permission to go out on dates, I must always go with a male chaperone and my sister and be home before 2am,' Shilpa explained. 'I cannot attend a party alone. And I'll never be allowed to go into my bedroom to be alone with a man; in fact, I would never hold a boyfriend's hand in front of my dad. It might sound funny to people here, but that's just the way it is with my family.'

Although her parents want her to marry, Shilpa is insistent they would never force her into something she wasn't happy with. 'Yes, many people in rural parts of India are very orthodox and have arranged marriages,' she told the paper. 'But I won't – I want to fall madly in love with someone and be whisked off my feet. Modern India is about metropolitan cities where people tend to be less culturally bound. So, although my parents are conservative, they're not that conservative and just want me to be with someone who will value me.

'They won't choose my husband but my parents' approval is very important to me. If I was really crazy about someone and they hated him, marriage wouldn't happen. Lately Mum and Dad have been putting pressure on me to marry, because it's relatively old to be single at 31. But I keep saying, "Please, not yet!" I don't want to go into a marriage just because of my age, too many people make that mistake. But of course I'd like to be married one day – I dream of having children because I adore kids so, so much.'

Of course, there was someone Shilpa had wanted to marry in the past and that came up again. Although she didn't name him, there was no doubt that she was talking about Akshay, and, even now, a hint of wistfulness was evident. 'I thought I would marry five years ago, but that relationship just didn't work out,' she admitted. 'I had my first boyfriend at 23, and fewer

Shilpa enjoys a night out with her mum at the *Music and Lyrics* film première.

beaten lonely and abused

BOYCOTT THE CIRCUS

Above: PETA (People for the Ethical Treatment of Animals) is a cause in which Shilpa believes passionately. Here, she promotes one of their campaigns.

Below: Shilpa was much in demand when she left the *Big Brother* house. She even visited the House of Commons as a guest of MP Keith Vaz.

Above: Bollywood comes to Berkshire. Shilpa filming with Salman Khan by the river in Reading.

Below: On top of the world – well, on top of her apartment block.

Above: Shilpa dancing at a concert organised in aid of earthquake relief.

© *Reuters*

Below: Shilpa's role as a high society escort girl in the film *Khamosh* was more daring than previous characters she'd played.   © *Reuters*/*Sherwin Crasto*

Above left: Bollywood stars get together to raise money for Indian tsunami victims. Shilpa is pictured here with Shah Rukh Khan.

© *Reuters/Punit Paranjpe*

Above right: Shilpa on the set of the film *Fareb*. She starred in this film with her sister, the only time they have appeared on screen together.

© *Reuters/Adeel Halim*

Below: Keeping it in the family. Shilpa with her sister Shamita and Manoj Bajpai, promoting *Fareb*.

© *Getty Images*

Shilpa's first big romance was with fellow Bollywood star Akshay Kumar.

Young, beautiful and intelligent – Shilpa now has the world at her feet.

© Jambala/ydimage.com/WENN

than five in my whole life. Every time I've fallen in love I've thought, "This is it," and every time I fall in love I feel more and more in love; I'm way too pragmatic to think true love only happens once. And I'm a pretty low-maintenance girlfriend – all I ask is that he buys me lots of diamonds!'

Shilpa had a good idea of the type of man she wanted to meet, although one result of her stay in the *Big Brother* household was that she was no longer necessarily looking for someone of the same nationality. 'My dream husband would be able to make me laugh, which isn't difficult,' she said. 'He'd respect my parents like his own and be financially well placed because I don't want any ego rifts. I would prefer to marry an Indian man, although meeting Jermaine in the house taught me people from abroad can also share my values and beliefs and don't have to be a no-no. I like David Beckham – I was going to say he is hot, but better say he's sweet because I admire Victoria so much. As for my wedding, it need not be a big sparkling event. I'd like a giant sparkling ring, but the event could be quite small.'

She also revealed quite how sheltered her background had been. 'My sister and I were only allowed to watch three hours of television a week, and always with my parents' supervision,' she said. 'So, when we were teenagers watching *Dallas* or *Dynasty* and a kissing scene was shown, we were expected to turn our faces from the screen. Mum and Dad always said, "Not until you are 17." So, when I made my first film at 17, called *Kiss Before Dying*, my first question to the director was: "Do I have to do kissing?" I was relieved when he said no because I didn't know how people did it.'

To put all of this in context, it is not just Shilpa who believes in modest appearance and demeanour, it's her entire country. And she herself has been prepared to tease the people she works with about the rigid moral stance everyone is expected to display; one famous anecdote in India shows she is more than capable of laughing at herself and everyone else.

It came about when she was filming *Metro*, with Shiney Ahuja. The director was Anurag Basu and, as much to pass the time as anything else, Shilpa, with the others present who were in on the secret, decided to play a trick. Everyone was at the Hotel Horizon at Juhu and, according to one source who was there, after Shilpa had finished the take for a song, clad in a long ethnic skirt, she went over to Anurag and said, 'I want to show you something.'

'Anurag thought maybe she had got some outfit or some accessory that she wanted to wear in the film that she wanted his opinion on,' said the source. 'But she mischievously started pulling down her skirt, leaving Anurag wondering what she was up to, in front of the whole unit. He was so embarrassed that he looked away till she called out to him.'

Shilpa, of course – as everyone else had known – was wearing jeans underneath. But it says something for Bollywood's culture that a director looks away when he thinks an actress is going to show him her legs. Standards of behaviour are different and actresses simply do not behave in the way they do in the West – and that applies to their private lives, as well.

Shilpa is quite aware of her appeal. For all the talk of not considering herself to be beautiful, there have been plenty of occasions on which she has not underestimated her charm. One interviewer put it to her head on: 'You're considered to have the best body in the industry,' he said. 'Ever seriously thought about that?'

'Yeah, I often wonder what they're thinking of when they say that,' said Shilpa. 'It's now become a status symbol to hit the gym. But in my case, I guess I'm just genetically blessed.'

'So who do you think has a better body?'

'Shiamak's troupe dancer Anisha has an amazing body. Technically speaking, my sister Shamita has a more ribbed physique.'

'What's your secret?'

'I have no workout regime, except for baithaks [a type of squat] and plunges – even those I haven't done in the last nine months. And I just love to eat. The one indulgence I have that is really fattening is chocolates. Since I suffer from low blood pressure, I have to keep popping them.'

A few years ago, she was asked, as she so often is, if marriage was on the cards. 'It will happen eventually, because I strongly believe in the institution,' said Shilpa. 'I'd love to be a mother someday. There's no such thing as the right man, but there certainly is a right moment, and that's what I'm waiting for. Marriage is a huge responsibility and I want to be 100 per cent ready for it. My husband will be my first priority; work will take a backseat initially.'

As for being linked with the people she worked with: 'As a newcomer, it was a culture shock for me, since I don't come from a filmi [sic] background,' she said. 'But now, I've realised it's the price you pay for being a celebrity. So I simply don't react to them now. As far as my conscience is clear, I'm OK. When I have a man to talk about, I'll do so openly.'

'Do you enjoy being looked upon as a sex symbol?'

'I take it as a huge compliment. There's nothing to feel apologetic about.'

Indeed, there wasn't. And Shilpa, as always, believed in looking ahead. There had been disappointments, personal and professional, but she had risen above it all with good grace. She had ignored the cattiness, got on with her life and only once, after the break-up with Akshay, had she allowed any private hurt to have a public face. Nor did she appear worried about the ageing process, remarking once, 'I'm like wine, I get better with age.' This was actually true. These days Shilpa is as beautiful as she has ever been and she knows how to present herself perfectly, too.

She has also learned there are certain subjects it's best not to talk about. 'I have had break-ups, but as a public figure I realise they are tougher to handle if you talk about them. Once you are seeing someone and the whole world knows about it, they want to know more – "Is it working out? Are they breaking up?" One of my biggest mistakes was to talk about my relationship with Akshay Kumar. After that I have kept everything to myself. Even when I was seeing Sandeep Chowta, neither of us spoke about it. Things didn't work out, but Sandeep and I respect each other, which is why we are still good friends.'

She was very much of the 'never complain' school of thought. 'I'm too positive a person to moan about the past,' she said. 'My positivity always overpowers my regrets. But I believe that everything is predestined, and everything, whether good or bad, is a learning experience.'

It was a wise philosophy, and one that has served her well. But men were not the only problems she had to contend with: surprisingly for a woman who once remarked, 'My mum is cooler than me,' Shilpa has managed to attract more than her fair share of controversy. Hers has been a life filled with incident, the stay in the *Big Brother* household simply being the most recent. Shilpa, the chaste Shilpa, has been publicly accused of obscenity, while her family was dragged into such a mire that on one occasion her father was actually arrested, although all charges against him were subsequently dropped. Indeed, far from *Big Brother* being the first time she has found herself in the midst of a furore, it is – at a conservative estimate and not counting the stories about the supposed men in her life, true or otherwise – at least the third occasion. It's no wonder she managed to stay calm in the face of Jade and co: in the past, she had been forced to endure far, far worse.

11
Nightmare

Bollywood was in shock: Shilpa Shetty was experiencing a nightmare. While she could do nothing but stand by and watch in horror, her much-loved father Surendra was arrested. He point blank denied the accusations levelled at him and was totally vindicated in due course. A tape recording relating to the incident, released at the time and reprinted below, was widely thought to be bogus. But it was a terrible time for the family, respected business people from Mumbai, and something no one could have forecast when Shilpa first burst on to the scene 10 years earlier.

The row related to events that took place in 1998. Shilpa had done some modelling for a company called

Praful Sarees and a dispute arose over her payment. It was claimed that she had only been paid the equivalent of about $113,000 out of a full fee of $679,000; the owner of Praful Sarees, Pankaj Agarwal, claimed the full sum had been paid in advance but that he didn't know what that payment was. Matters came to a head in May 2003, when DK Gupta, the Police Commissioner of Surat, announced Praful Sarees had lodged complaints with them after receiving threatening phone calls from Indian underworld figures demanding the money be paid in full. A warrant was issued for both parents' arrest on charges of extortion and a tape recording released. It should be emphasised that, as the investigation was to subsequently establish, neither of Shilpa's parents or anyone associated with her had authorised this conversation, and someone was clearly out to cause serious trouble for the Shettys.

The transcript of the tape, which was transliterated and translated by Rediff in May 2003, is as follows. The transcript has been edited for legal reasons:

Caller: *Shilpa Shetty wala matter hai.* [This is about the Shilpa Shetty matter.]
Agarwal: *Kya matter? Kaisa matter? Aap kaun bol rahe hai?* [What matter? Who is speaking?]

Caller: *Acchha, tu ek kaam kar, bhai se baat kar le.*
[OK, speak to 'bhai'.]

(He gives Man A's number and disconnects. Man A phones Agarwal.)

Man A: *Apko unko do khokha dena padenga.* [You have to pay them Rs 2 crore.]
Agarwal: *Lekin hamara kuch lena-dena nahin nikalta.* [But I don't owe them anything.]
Man A: *Aapko bata diya na, aapko paisa dena hi padenga.* [I have told you, you have to give the money.]

(The original caller rings again.)

Caller: *Aap ne kya socha?* [What have you decided?]
Agarwal: *Lekin hamara kuch lena-dena nahin hai.* [But I have nothing to do with them.]
Caller: A*apse paisa vasool karne ke liye hamein advance bhi mil gaya hai. Agar paisa nahin diya to hum tumhara game kar denge.* [We have already received an advance to get the money from you. If you do not pay up, we will kill you.]
Agarwal: *Lekin aap ke aadmi ho kaise maloom padenga?* [How will I know if you are the man?]

Caller: *Main aapko ek number deta hoon, aap wahan baat kar lena.* [I will give you a number. Speak to them.]

(He gives a telephone number.)

(Agarwal calls Man B on the number given to him by the caller.)

Agarwal: *Aap bhi businessman ho. Main bhi hoon. Yeh raasta barabar nahin hai. Woh log to apni zabaan mein baat karte hain. Woh seedhi baat nahin karte.* [Both of us are businessmen. This tactic is not good. Those people do not deal properly, they use their own language.]

Man B: *Aap ko paisa to dena hi padenga.* [You will have to pay up.]

(Man B gives Agarwal another number to call)

Agarwal: 'Man A' *mujhe bahut pareshan karta hai. Main office mein baith nahin sakta hoon, aap please use rokiye.* [Man A is harassing me. I cannot sit in my office. Please stop him.]

Man C: *Aap humko paisa de do, phones apne aap hi*

band ho jayenge. [Give us the money. The telephone calls will stop.]

Bollywood could not believe it. Akshay Kumar, no less, made his own feelings quite clear: 'I'm shocked beyond words. Shilpa's parents are too decent to be involved with all this. It's incredible.'

His view was widely shared by the film world, while Shilpa herself could hardly believe it. 'I have never harmed anyone in my 10 years in the industry,' she said. 'I don't know why I've been targeted this way. What really hurts is that my parents are being hurt. Why them? God is witness to what's happening to us. I'll wait for justice to prevail.'

The timing of it all was also very odd. Allegations began to surface when Shilpa was at the high-profile IIFA awards at South Africa and matters reached a head when she headed a dance festival at Cannes. This was her first big exposure to the West and, if someone had sat down and worked out the worst possible time for the allegations to surface, they couldn't have done better than this. The Shettys, certainly, were convinced someone was out to harm them. In June that year, Sunanda held a press conference in which she pointblank denied the allegations and added that it was a 'plot to tarnish the image of my daughter'.

Several contradictory stories emerged. There were accounts stating Surendra had confessed to the police that he'd met Fazl-ur-Rehman, the leader of the gang; at the same time it was reported he'd denied the meeting. The latter turned out to be true. In a further complication, the man said to have arranged the meeting, Dilip Pashekar, was the Shettys' driver and he too was eventually arrested that November. In June 2003, Surendra was formally arrested following reports of cell-phone records linking him to the gang. He protested, 'I don't know, I talked to them only after they called up and said they were agents of Agarwal.' It was a mess.

Shilpa arrived back in the middle of it all and denied any involvement whatsoever in the case. Her mother had power of attorney over her money and she had no knowledge at all about any of the figures involved. She became increasingly upset as matters developed, feeling that her family was being subjected to trial by media: 'I was shocked at the media's irresponsible behaviour,' she said later. 'It was very difficult for me to do any damage control. They made a mountain of a molehill because of which the entire thing was blown out of proportion. The news broke out last year while I was performing at the IIFA awards in South Africa. When I went on stage I knew that everyone was going to concentrate on my state of mind instead of my performance. Later, the media just pounced on me, asking me about all that happened in Mumbai. It is in the past now, and I have grown even closer to my family now.'

But the experience left its mark. 'I am basically a happy, positive person,' she said on another occasion. 'But I have my fears, such as that I may not be there for my parents when they need me the most. I experienced that and worse when there was a case against us. I have watched my father, a respected white-collared senior citizen, who hasn't so much as hurt a fly in his entire life, being roughed up by policemen. In spite of being a celebrity, I was not able to do anything. It was a nightmare; I was completely helpless. I have managed to put that incident behind me and I hope nothing like this ever happens again.'

It was a very unpleasant experience indeed, and one for which the family was totally unprepared. But it also rather puts the events in the *Big Brother* house in context: Shilpa had experienced considerably worse than that. She said she was 'very cut up' and 'devastated', and the ramifications of the case sometimes seemed endless. In August 2006, Fazl-ur-Rehman was arrested, something that made Sunanda declare publicly that Shilpa had no connection with the case and that the arrest would have nothing to do with her career. Shilpa continued to talk about how upsetting it was, and publicly thanked several figures in the Indian film industry for standing by her, most notably Rajkumar Santoshi and Anil Kapoor.

But that was not the end of controversial matters for Shilpa. Three years later, in 2006, she had to live through another nightmare, this time of a very different kind. In April 2006, a Madurai court issued non-bailable warrants against Shilpa and another actress, Reema Sen, for 'posing in an obscene manner' for pictures in a Tamil newspaper. According to the petitioner, the paper had published 'very sexy blow-ups and medium blow-ups' in its issues in December 2005 and January 2006 which, according to the petitioner, violated the Indecent Representation of Women (Prohibition) Act 1986, Young Persons (Harmful Publications) Act 1956 and the Indian Penal Code Section 292 (Sale of Obscene Books) and the two actresses had failed to comply with earlier summonses for the same reason.

Shilpa was outraged and showed as much in her response. For a start, she said, she'd never received any previous summons. Second, the pictures in question were freeze-frame shots from *Auto Shankar*, a Kannada film (a film in which the Kannada language is spoken) she'd made, co-starring Upendra. Furthermore, the pictures only showed her navel. 'As far as my photographs go, what is obscene about it?' she demanded. 'If navel-showing is obscenity, then our traditional Indian outfit – the traditional sari – should be banned in the first place!'

She also, rather understandably, felt there were more important issues in the world to worry about than pictures of her wearing a sari. 'I think there are more important and crucial issues that need to be tackled,' she commented. 'Such issues certainly don't deserve headlines. And frankly, I haven't received any summons from the court. Even if something like this happens, I have full faith in our judiciary.'

Her irritation, given that she had not actually posed for the pictures, and that they were stills from a film, was understandable. 'It's a democratic country,' she said. 'What I do is my concern as long as I know where to draw the line and not offend anybody. As far as my photographs go, what is obscene about it?'

Asked how she defined obscenity, Shilpa replied, 'It is the way one perceives it. Sometimes, shooting in the rain can look obscene if it is not shot aesthetically. Or a short skirt can look sexy, if it's shot in a tasteful way. It depends on certain camera angles ... I am a responsible citizen with prudent thoughts. One doesn't have to look sexy for the heck of it; it all depends on the subject of the movie. There's a thin line between vulgarity and sensuality, and I have never crossed that. I have always been praised for aesthetic sensibilities when it comes to exposing.'

To reinforce the point, she approached the National Commission for Women (NCW), who supported her fully. 'When the Censor Board has cleared her film for public viewing, where does the question of obscenity arise?' demanded Dr Girija Vyas, chairperson of the NCW.

Her fellow actress Reema Sen was none too pleased either. 'The legal system should take up bigger and better social issues like protecting women's rights rather than targeting celebs,' she said. 'Actresses have to be decently dressed as they influence the public, but it doesn't give anybody the right to act as the moral police.'

Dale Bhagwagar, Shilpa's spokesman, said, 'On

behalf of my client, Shilpa Shetty, I hereby clarify that she hasn't received any legal "summons" or "warrant", as misreported by a section of the media. I would like to state here that this is not a photo-shoot picture for which Shilpa has posed, neither can it be termed as one to offend sensibilities. She's being made a scapegoat, paying the price for being a celebrity.'

He later enlarged upon this, adding, 'There has been indiscriminate misreporting in the media, which has given undue national importance to this frivolous case. This tarnished Shilpa Shetty's clean image. Ms Shetty is not only hurt over the case filed against her, but is also feeling targeted, hassled and victimised by it. She is a responsible actress and citizen and would never participate in anything crude.'

He had a very good point, and by this time Shilpa was showing signs of being tired of being targeted in this way. The High Court issued a stay warrant on the proceedings, but, even so, the papers remained obsessed with Shilpa's various travails. Why, she was asked, was she at the centre of so much controversy? 'Yeah, even I don't know why,' she admitted in 2006. 'I'm in the news for the strangest reasons and there are quite a few of them actually. I think the media has just gone berserk, there's hardly any consistency in their reporting. Certain cases of mine are *sub judice*, so I can't comment on them. But the print and electronic media keeps putting ideas in the minds of readers and viewers which can be quite harmful.'

The case caused a furore in a way that is almost impossible to understand in the West. *The Times* of India, no less, joined the debate, musing on how obscenity was defined these days. Supreme Court lawyer Alpana Poddar joined in. 'Obscenity is a wide word,' she said. 'It changes with time. What was considered obscene 20 years ago is not considered so now.' She did, however, have a rather novel reason for feeling that these cases should come up before a court: 'Otherwise, they just might go around indulging in vandalism, burning down theatres or publishing houses.'

But Shilpa had clearly been very hurt by a great deal that had been written. 'I am very upset,' she said. 'I would request the media to get their facts right before saying or writing something. There are serious issues in our country which need attention but every day I see only trivial matters being reported. There's a limit to fluff and fabrications. I just want the media to address issues intelligently … Look, I'm in the film industry for the last 13 years. I just don't have the energy to clarify my stand to the media – I want to do quality work. Full stop! Giving interviews has become a harrowing experience for me. Moreover, the press reports news according to their convenience. When there was a non-bailable warrant against me in the obscenity case, they put it on the front page. But, when the High Court issued a stay order on the warrant, it was published as a small news item on page seven. These things have disturbed me a lot.'

Indeed, she was not going to let anyone get away with this. Always outspoken about what she thought and believed in, she had no intention of being quiet now. Apart from anything else, there was a good deal of outrage that she had been singled out in this way: she was, after all, no different from any other Bollywood actress and to be picked upon, particularly in the wake of the charges against her parents, was not on. Nor was this the first time she had been accused of vulgarity – in the early days of her film career some of her dance sequences had attracted exactly the same criticism – although it was certainly the first occasion when she was faced with legal proceedings. Enough was enough.

'It [the photo] is not vulgar,' she said. 'I am an actor and an entertainer and I won't endorse vulgarity. I always do everything in a dignified manner. And tell me, have I done anything that other actresses have not done? With God's grace, work is going fine. But this is definitely affecting our reputation. In my family, everybody has worked hard for small little success. We are law-abiding citizens, we won't do anything unlawful.'

Again, she was sick of the media. Like so many stars, in Bollywood and in the West, she had a tough dilemma: she needed the press to some degree to maintain the public's interest in her, and yet, when their coverage became intrusive and unpleasant, she wanted a break. Certainly, her family had been on the end of more than its fair share of negative publicity in recent years so it was hardly surprising that she was annoyed. 'I don't like the way the media is focusing on such inane issues. They are making a mountain out of a molehill,' she said.

Unusually, and to illustrate just how fed up she was, Shilpa had written to the Chief Justice of India, YK Sabharwal. She was seeking, she said, a guiding precedent in 'maligning cases' by lawyers against film artistes. 'It's not that the Chief Justice is going to write a reply to me,' she continued. 'But I have full faith in the judiciary and I am sure something positive will come out. The case is in the court. Legal proceedings take time in our country.'

She could also hardly believe she had been accused of obscenity; after all, this is the woman who has reacted badly to speculation about her private life. 'The problem in our country is that the judiciary is seriously overworked, PILs [Public Interest Litigations] make it even tougher for them,' she said. 'I respect our judiciary which has no option but to respond to these PILs. I don't know if it will ever stop, I can just hope and wait.'

Sometimes it seemed the scrutiny was endless to the extent that even the mildest of incidents could get out of hand. On yet another occasion, it was reported that Shilpa's mother had been involved in a spat with the press. 'Oh, that was totally blown out of proportion,' responded Shilpa, rather wearily, to questioning. 'I was in Kolkata for a promotional event for *Shaadi Karke Phas Gaya Yaar*. There was complete chaos at the event with hordes of cameramen and photographers. And there was this guy who hit my mum on her lower hip to come forward to click my pictures. I don't blame my mum, it was a reflex action which anyone would have taken. She just turned back and pushed the guy away. In that moment of anger, she asked the man to behave himself. Later, of course, he apologised and that was that.'

This, then, is the background Shilpa emerged from to take up the challenge of the *Big Brother* house. She had already been put to the test more than once and had always risen above it, no matter how hurtful or upsetting the circumstances might have been. Add to this the various fictitious reports surrounding her private life, to say nothing of the long fight she had endured to even get recognised in Bollywood, and it's clear she is made of stern stuff.

As she herself has acknowledged, she is also remarkably balanced, something else that emerged after her stint in the *Big Brother* house. After coming out, and before her press conference, she was assessed by a professional to make sure she was unscathed by it all. 'I saw the psychologist and he was showing me all the clippings but I was trying to do my make-up,' said Shilpa. 'Finally, he said, "You don't need me – you're just too grounded."'

It was, of course, a result of her warm and secure family background.

Even so, all this did not put her off supporting worthy causes and giving a little back. Shilpa is one of the actresses who supports PETA (People for the

Ethical Treatment of Animals), although she doesn't do so in the way of her Western counterparts, namely, by posing naked against posters reading, 'I'd rather go naked than wear fur.' Instead, she provides fully clothed support, but is nonetheless prepared to do her bit to shock people out of complacency.

In 2006, in the wake of a horrible incident in Mumbai, in which 21 animals belonging to a Russian circus were burned alive, Shilpa took part in a campaign to dissuade people from going to circuses that use live animals. She dressed in a tight catsuit, covered in animal strikes, her face made up with whiskers, and was confined to a small cage, in pictures shot by the famous Indian photographer Atul Kasbekar. The caption on the picture read: 'Beaten, lonely and abused – boycott the circus.' It was a cause close to Shilpa's heart: 'By no means was I comfortable during the photo shoot crouched in that small cage,' she remarked. 'But what were a few fleeting moments of discomfort for me compared to what life must be like for the precious animals held captive in the circus? These once dignified animals only leave their cages, which are barely larger than the size of their bodies, for a few minutes each day to be forced into the ring to perform tricks which make no sense and are upsetting to them. The best way to help animals suffering in circuses is to boycott the circus.'

A long-time animal lover, although not actually a vegetarian herself, Shilpa was passionate about her concern for animals. 'I feel very strongly towards this cause,' she said. 'There is too much injustice happening towards animals. My entire family loves animals; our pets at home are family. I was appalled when I came to know what atrocities animals are subjected to in the circuses. I thought I should stop that. If I can make a little difference to their lives, why not go for it?'

PETA was very grateful for her involvement in the campaign and, just over six months later, when they saw what she was being subjected to in the *Big Brother* house, they repaid the compliment. 'When Shilpa did her advertisement against circuses for PETA, she had no idea that she would eventually be living in the midst of one,' said a PETA spokesman, as uproar raged. 'We encourage everyone to vote for Shilpa in tomorrow night's show.'

It was very nicely put. But then Shilpa hadn't played it safe in other areas, either. With so much going on in her private life, she could have been forgiven for forgetting about the professional aspect of things, but she was as focused on her career as ever. And she was prepared to make bold choices in her film roles, too. Having proved that she really could act as well as dance and look pretty, she started to take on action roles – it was now that the Indian media dubbed her the Eastern answer to Angelina Jolie, and there was even speculation that she might star in an Indian version of Lara Croft – to say nothing of making a very bold choice of film. In a country that still shunned talking about such things, Shilpa very bravely chose to play a woman suffering from HIV – and it was a choice that would pay off.

12

Not Just Lashes
and Lipstick

One of the great ironies of Shilpa's career to date is that, every time she finally seems to have made her breakthrough, and to be regarded as a fine actress rather than just a glamour girl, something happens to knock her back again. Often it has simply been a slew of bad films, but, just as Bollywood seemed to be taking her seriously, the court case involving her parents blew up, rather overshadowing everything else. And indeed, Shilpa stopped making so many films at this point, although she was adamant this was her own choice. From now on, she declared, her film choices were going to be based on quality, not quantity.

'Definitely. I lay a very conscious effort on selecting

just quality-based movies,' she said. 'But it is indeed very difficult rejecting movies, keeping in mind the best roles and interesting films that I am being offered at this stage of my career. I had initially decided to act in just two films in a year but, as things stand, I already have three to four films at hand. I definitely want to do things that justify me as a character; I really don't intend to typecast myself. The audience has been really kind to me and I have been receiving feedback from them regarding my good work.'

She conceded that she had good reason to stay away from the press. 'Can you blame me?' she asked. 'But I wasn't shying away from media though I was upset with them, besides I didn't have much to say. But today it's all in the past. I was treated as a public figure would have been, yet it hurt to be called names and given unjust tags. It wasn't fair. I am sure the judicial system will dole out justice, though it takes a while. That topic brings back horrible memories. My parents were dragged into the mess simply because I'm a celebrity. The whole incident has made me stronger as a person. Now I can handle anything.'

Not, of course, that she had been entirely absent from the silver screen – appearances included the films *Darna Manaa Hai* and *Karz* – she was just slightly less conspicuous than previously. But that was about to change. Shilpa appeared in three films in quick succession opposite the same leading man, Salman Khan, in three totally different roles, which once and for all proved to the cynics that she could not just act, but she also had range. She also appeared in several others at around the same time.

Clearly she felt she had something to prove. 'My critics have always tried to write me off,' said Shilpa, just before all the films were due to be released. 'But I've always kept quiet. They say there is always a lull before the storm. Now I've come with a big bang. I have four releases. There is *Garv*, *Phir Milenge*, *Khamosh* and *Dus*. I am waiting for meatier roles. I have done enough song and dance sequences – I have nothing against them, I cannot forget that that's how I became Shilpa Shetty. I cannot take that away, I have done *jhatkas* and *matkas*, but now I want to do meatier roles (to put it the right way). I feel I have more potential and I want to tap it.'

The first of these films, *Phir Milenge*, was a genuinely brave choice. It tackled the subject of HIV – still a difficult one in Western cinemas, never mind Bollywood – and showed Shilpa in a new and very different light.

Shilpa, who played a woman with HIV, was very keen to talk about her forthcoming role. 'Why not a film on HIV-positive patients?' she asked. 'It is a social stigma in our society. We made this film to highlight this problem. It is not preachy, it is a very sweet love story. It is the journey of these characters Abhishek [Bachchan], Salman [Khan] and me, in the midst of which the spectre of this HIV positive pops up. I keep emphasising HIV positive because I didn't know the difference between HIV positive and AIDS. AIDS and HIV positive *mein zameen aasman ka farak hai* [There is a world of a difference between the two]. This film will bring about a social awareness about AIDS in our country. It is high time we talked about this in our society. Remember, there was a stigma associated with tuberculosis earlier? But that has changed with time, hasn't it?'

She was enjoying the fact that she now had more control over what she did. 'I have become selective because I can afford to,' she said. 'I want to do meatier roles. It is always great to be glamorous. I have enjoyed the *jhatka-matkas* in all my films. I want to balance that with films like *Phir Milenge* but there is another problem: if you do serious films, people think you are only open to arty films. I want to strike a balance between the *jhatka-matka* and serious films. I feel more confident after *Phir Milenge*. *Dhadkan* changed people's attitude towards me. People felt I couldn't fit into other characters, but *Dhadkan* proved them wrong.'

Indeed, so keen had she been to do the film that she accepted considerably less than her usual fee. 'Let me put it this way,' she said. 'There are some films that you do for money and some for creative satisfaction. *Phir Milenge* belongs to the latter category. When Revathi came to meet me in Mysore and narrated the storyline of the film, I took it up for two reasons – one, the story excited me immensely and, two, since I had watched her previous film *Mitr*, I wanted to work with her some day. When she said that she had budget constraints and that she could offer me an "X" amount, I didn't want to let go of this opportunity just because price was an issue. Believe me, *Phir Milenge* will give me tremendous respect as an actor.'

In the making of the film, Shilpa also had to do something many actresses dread – appear without make-up. 'The film centres around a smart, independent working woman who finds herself in a predicament,' she said. 'It's quite different from what I have done to date. The role is realistically portrayed. I appeared without make-up in the second half of the film, as required. It was a challenging role for I've always appeared glamorous all my life and Revathi was strict about it too. After *Phir Milenge*, I understood that outfits and looks are not that essential as living a character totally. Revathi taught me that and many more things. She is quite a talented and lively person, and working with Salman and Abhishek was terrific.

'The best thing about *Phir Milenge* is that Revathi refused to let me apply make-up throughout the making of the film. In fact, I couldn't recognise myself when I watched the monitor after every take on the sets. The character of Tamanna is like real life on celluloid. It is a very identifiable character. In real life, no woman wears pink eyeliners and shadow. Revathi did not want anything that would have looked unreal in her film.'

As with her work for PETA, Shilpa felt this was her way of giving something back. 'It is one important message that we all have to believe in,' she said. 'The stigma that has become synonymous with the disease has to be done away with. Through *Phir Milenge*, I have been able to do my bit as an entertainer. The film's box-office fate doesn't really matter; the message should reach the audiences. Once the promos came on air, there was so much positive feedback. I have always been lauded for my dances but here were people calling me up and telling me that they loved the way I cried!'

In the event, she was nominated for Best Actress for the film by a number of award ceremonies, although in the event she failed to win. 'I am someone who is totally disillusioned by awards, but in all fairness and honesty, it would be very encouraging to win an award after so many years of hard work,' said Shilpa. 'And I am not disillusioned because I haven't won an award, but because I find many a time a deserving person doesn't get it. That hurts me, because I know how much effort goes into filmmaking and acting. I hope *Phir Milenge* gets its due because that will create an interest in the film and help people realise its message.'

But the film was certainly not all Shilpa was working on. Shortly before it came out, she starred in *Garv*, a much more typically glamorous role for her. 'I play a Muslim orphan,' she explained. 'Her name is Jannat. She is a bar dancer. She admires the hero, Salman Khan, because of his integrity. She thinks all men look at her as a body, but this man treats her like a human being.'

Asked if she did any research before taking on the role, she replied, 'Not really. This is not a very serious role like Tabu's in *Chandni Bar*. It [*Garv*] is essentially a cop drama. My character is involved with the hero. We have concentrated on that; we have not concentrated on the turmoil that goes on in her life.'

Nor did she make any particularly extravagant claims about her role, and it is a mark of her self-confidence that she was able to talk like this. You wouldn't get many Western actresses playing down their role in the way she did here. 'I play Salman's love interest in the film,' she continued. 'It's a hard-hitting cop drama. I cannot go on and on about my role because it is a male-dominated film. I'm not here to make an impact – my songs and dance will do the talking. I did the film because it's a very big production; Salman's a dear friend. Besides, Puneet approached me and I could not refuse. They wanted a dancer and, since I love dancing, I said yes. I had nothing to lose, it's a good film.'

After *Garv* came *Khamosh*. Directed by Deepak Tijori, this is a thriller starring Shilpa, Shawar Ali and Rajeev Singh in principal roles with another of the type of numbers that had made her famous, '*Mera Tan Bola Mera Man Bola*'. Shilpa had rather a daring role. 'I am playing the character of a very high-society escort girl who is quite sophisticated and presentable,' she said. 'I accepted the script as soon as the director narrated the script to me because it's a kind of movie that has never been made before and Deepak's setting and presentation of the movie is so superb that even our audience would really enjoy the movie. The movie is a psychological thriller that revolves around six different characters and what happens to them in the course of one night. The movie seems to be very interesting and the character that I am playing in *Khamosh* is very different from what I have played before.'

According to Shilpa, this was not, however, a return to the kind of films she had made in the past; it was a good deal more sophisticated. 'The presentation of this movie is very realistic,' she said. 'It's not a musical film. But the movie has a superb background score, which indeed is an integral part of the script. [The song] happens at an interesting juncture, which is the most important day in the life of this materialistic girl. This girl does something in the midst of this song and, immediately after she leaves, her life takes a turning point.

'The interesting aspect of the movie is that the shoot will be over within 30 days. Since we all are not shooting for five films at one time, all the characters in the movie will be very much involved in its scripting providing the necessary crispness without switching the characters every now and then. The film happens only at nights and that necessitates the film to be shot only at nights. It's really different for me to work on a script like *Khamosh*.'

In the event, alas, the film did not do particularly well.

Next up was a movie called *Dus*, which started the comparisons with Angelina Jolie and on which she met Anubhav. Shilpa was extremely flattered by the comparison to Angelina. 'If you think I am a match for Angelina Jolie, that is huge! Thanks!' she said to a journalist. 'But I like to believe that the character has more of Shilpa Shetty and less of Jolie's pout. On a serious note, what excited me most was that I would be doing action that hasn't been attempted before by Bollywood heroines. And the action in *Dus* isn't the ordinary fare, it is slick and fast.'

Indeed, Shilpa was playing no ordinary Bollywood heroine. 'I am doing *Dus* because my character is very unconventional,' she said. 'I am playing an anti-terrorist squad member. I wear holsters, use guns and my hair is all tied up. I don't look pretty in the film, I look tough. It is a meaty role and has given me the chance to reinvent myself. I am now looking for roles that are different – I want more paradigm shifts in my role.'

It was certainly very different from anything she had done before. 'One day when I reported to the sets, Allan Amin was sitting there with his set-up all ready,' she said. 'I walked up to him and asked, "Who's doing action today, Sanju or Suniel?"

'"You are," he said.

'"Are you crazy? I can't do that, it's impossible!" I screamed.

'Allan said, "I am here to make the impossible possible."

'He just got me, packed me into the costume and we got cracking. Now, when I look back I am so glad that he pushed me into doing it, and, more importantly, I am thankful that he believed that a heroine could pull it off!'

Of course, in Bollywood, it was men who were used to doing the action sequences, but on this film Shilpa received nothing but support from her male co-stars. 'Actually, Sanju was very supportive of me doing action,' she said. 'It's been absolutely marvellous. The entire concept of a woman doing action appealed to me a great deal. And the boys have been very gung-ho about us girls sharing guns and thrills. And, after seeing the rushes, I don't think I have done too bad!'

And what, she was asked, did she make of Anubhav

Sinha? 'Nah, he isn't this stern and strict guy that people make him out to be,' she remarked. 'When I landed on the first day of the shoot, I looked around and saw that there was no video assist [to check on shots]. When I asked Anubhav about it, he said, "It's a mere waste of time, I trust you, Shilpa, and know that you will deliver the goods." To know that your director trusts you come what may is such a revelation for an artist. Besides, Anubhav is so "sure" about things that I doubt if a machine can improve that!'

So, was Shilpa now a 'serious' actress rather than a glamour puss? '"Serious", "glamorous", "arty", these are just labels that the media hounds me with,' she responded wearily. 'For me, I am an actor and my job is to throw caution to the wind and do any and every role that excites me. I am very clear that I want to be associated with cinema that is entertaining and interesting, period. The rest is just tabloid junkie, it doesn't matter. [*Dus*] is a complete entertainer. The film is super-slick and extremely stylised. I recently saw the rushes and was blown away! I am so proud to be associated with something as huge as *Dus*. It's shot on a grand scale; don't try to catch it on a DVD or your telly, this one's a big-screen experience for sure! You'll love it!'

By now, the films were flooding in thick and fast. The next on the cards was *Fareb*, also starring Shamita, to date the only time sisters have appeared together in a Bollywood film. 'Both my recent releases tapped more than just my dancing potential,' said Shilpa. 'In *Dus*, I actually do stunts. That one kick I pulled off has been so widely noticed! I can't believe the impact. And in *Fareb*, Shamita and I are the only sisters in Hindi cinema to have appeared together. Isn't that cool?'

Indeed, she appeared to be delighted to be working with Shamita. 'Forget Jennifer and Angelina, why are people comparing Shamita with me? Let me tell you, my sister is far hotter than me!' she said. 'The way she has performed her tough role in *Fareb* is breathtaking. She has just started, and I feel she has a very bright career – I'm so proud of her.'

There were rumours that a film had been made starring two sisters as a clever ruse on Shilpa's part. 'Wrong!' she said. 'They went to her first – she didn't want to do it. Then, after they signed me for the other role as Manoj Bajpai's wife, they went back to her. This time she agreed, and not because I agreed. And, please, I didn't do *Fareb* for my sister's career! We've equal roles – she's there throughout the first half while I take over in the second half. Fifty-fifty.'

Nor was there any rivalry between the two. 'Rather than labelling it as sibling rivalry or professional rivalry, I would like to call this healthy competition,' said Shilpa. 'Healthy competition is always very good and it always enhances a performance. It was a fun experience, an exciting experience, other than the fact that the film for us is like a casting coup. The USP of this film is definitely the performances – all the artists in the film have given very nice performances, this is the film I am proud of. It was a difficult role for Shamita, but she has carried it beautifully, Manoj, as always, has given an astounding performance. I, too, to an extent have tried to match up to his performance. What I have learned from Shamita is that she is so much more patient than me and she is a complete stickler for perfection. I am someone who to a certain extent would compromise but she is someone who believes that you shouldn't compromise in life.'

As ever, she was keen to talk about her role in the film. 'My character is that of the doctor named Neha, who is also a devoted wife,' she said. 'So, if I have to describe this woman in one line, I think she is the ideal Indian woman, someone who balances her work and her family very well. I think I would love to be someone like Neha – she is very simple and a thoughtful person.

She is someone very humane and that is something her husband also admires her for; it's a very sweet, very nice character.'

Fareb was, in fact, directed by Deepak Tijori, who had also done *Khamosh*. Given the latter hadn't done very well, how did Shilpa feel about working with him again? 'Deepak is a very dear friend and I know people question *Fareb* as a film, after *Khamosh* not doing well, but I think it is unfair. I'd like to stand up for him and say that he has done a very good job in *Fareb*,' she responded firmly. 'It's very unfair for people to be so judgemental depending on your last film. Everyone makes good films and bad films, but it's OK, it's just part of the game. But I am proud of him: as a maker he has come into his own in this film, he's really made something he has believed in. It's always been a pleasure working with him.

'I had never thought that I would do one after other film with Deepak, but, when I was doing *Khamosh*, Deepak came with the script of *Fareb* and I very unwillingly read it. But, when I read the script, I totally loved the characterisation; they were something we could relate to in real life. All we are trying to show is that it's only human to commit mistakes, nobody is a god. We have just tried to capture human emotion on celluloid.'

There was music in this one, about which Shilpa was as keen as ever. 'I really like *Fareb*'s music because all the songs are situational and lyrically also they are very nice,' she said. 'There is a romantic track, a disco number, a remix number, which I am sure is going to rock all the pubs. I think that I have been very lucky with music and, whatever film of mine Anu has given music for, all have been a hit. Even in this film there is Baras Ja, then there is also a romantic number sung by Kunal Ganjawala.

'There are a lot of emotions [in the film] projected on different levels, which makes this film very interesting. Of a husband who is betraying his wife, who is also feeling bad while doing so, then of the wife who is totally unaware of what is happening, emotions of the other woman who wants this man completely. So there is a gamut of emotions this film is packed with. Shamita is also a brilliant dancer, which she has proved in her previous films. *Fareb* is a great amalgamation of a thriller with a love story.'

In the event, *Fareb* was rather overshadowed by *Dus*, which was released at the same time. 'The bigger film got the bigger opening,' said a philosophical Shilpa in the aftermath. 'We had gone to a multiplex to watch *Dus*. While coming out, we came across people who had just seen *Fareb*. They all came forward to say how much they liked the film.'

And in retrospect, Shilpa clearly thought that working as they had done on *Khamosh* hadn't been such a good idea after all. 'Too many constraints,' she said. 'We had to finish the film in 25 days. Do you know *Khamosh* was the first film where I was paired with a newcomer? Right from my first film – *Baazigar* – I've co-starred only with the top guns, except Ajay Devgan, with whom I've never worked. I wonder why!'

But it was *Dus* that she was particularly proud of, along with its director, Anubhav Sinha. 'I love the way he used me in the film, not as a glamour prop but as a character who carries the script forward,' said Shilpa. 'I was professional and yet I had a love life. Not too many heroines play such a character. I love the way Anubhav co-ordinated the large number of characters. It's a very difficult job to keep balance in a film where the number of characters is so high. I knew *Fareb* would be crushed by *Dus*. Anubhav Sinha's film is much bigger and with far bigger stars, though stars no longer ensure a hit. I feel *Fareb* is a decent marital drama. Besides, it gave me a chance to work with my sister.'

Following that frankly impressive run of films, Shilpa decided to take another break. 'And by choice,' she said to an interviewer at the time. 'At this very moment, I've four scripts on hand, but I don't think I'll do any of them – I'd rather stay at home than do films I don't believe in.'

In fact, one of her biggest challenges to date would soon be on the cards. Shilpa was soon to do some television in India, but after that there would be the show that was to make her an international name. All that was still to come, however. For now, she was just Shilpa Shetty, glamour girl turned serious actress.

13

Television Beckons

The world of showbusiness was agog. Shilpa Shetty, the actress whose career had taken more turns than an Alpine highway, was about to embark upon yet another phase in her career. And, as with so much to do with Shilpa, hardly had it been announced than it was already mired in controversy. But this was not *Big Brother* – far from it. This was a show made in India by Sony entitled *Jhalak Dikhla Jaa*, a new dance show, and Shilpa was to take part as a judge, although a report had upset both Shilpa and the music channel by saying that she had replaced someone else, Karisma Kapoor, in the role. It was hardly the auspicious introduction to television she had wanted and she was not slow to snap back.

'This paper has been targeting me on the smallest of pretexts,' she fumed. 'They called me a jobless actress, which I am not for sure. I currently have two major films on the floor. I know the truth about why I've stepped into *Jhalak Dikhla Jaa* and how much I've been paid. I see no reason to tom-tom my career moves to people who are hellbent on writing me off! If people see my debut on television as a downslide in my career, I can't help it. Let me remind them I'm not doing a soap.'

Indeed, this was not the first time she had an offer to appear on the small screen. 'I've been offered lots of television shows before,' she said. 'So far, I resisted the temptation because I didn't want anyone to say I was getting into television because I had no films on hand. It's another matter that even now I'm being subjected to barbs about being jobless. Right now, I'm working on Anurag Basu's *Metro*, where I've a role to die for.

'If I've chosen to cut down on films it's only because I can't do crappy parts at this stage of my career. I'd rather do *Jhalak Dikhla Jaa* on TV, where I get to be part of something I enjoy unconditionally – dancing.'

In fact, Shilpa had done television work before, albeit briefly, when she appeared as a guest judge on *Indian Idol* in 2004, but the experience was to prove invaluable in handling herself on television. And the rumours that she wasn't costing as much as other actresses became deeply ironic in light of what she was to be paid to go on *Big Brother* and the numerous opportunities it would open up for her. Her willingness to try out a new route simply demonstrated what had come up in her career time and again: that she was prepared to take risks, try out new projects and see where new roads took her. It was an approach that was to pay off spectacularly well.

And Anupama Mandloi, spokesman for Sony, was keen to defend their star. 'We did have a problem with Karisma and we did ask Shilpa to step in,' he said. 'But to suggest that she has been paid a meagre amount is a joke.'

'I've been around long enough not to get insecure about less work now,' Shilpa added philosophically. 'I've seen many girls come and go. By God's grace, I'm still around and in a position to do the kind of work that I really enjoy. The best part of doing *Jhalak Dikhla Jaa* is my colleagues, who are Farah Khan and Sanjay Leela Bhansali. I've never worked with either, but I've always admired their work.'

But the programme certainly was not launching without problems. Even after the problems with

Karisma, there was more uncertainty about who was to take part, after the composer Himesh Reshammiya pulled out.

'We asked him to compose the title song for us. He wanted to be paid the sun, moon and stars. We reeled under his remunerative demands and quickly went to Vishal-Shekhar, who has composed a beautiful signature tune for us. Javed Akhtar has written the song,' said Mandoli. 'Sure, it has the words "*jhalak dikhla jaa*" in it. But our song is completely different from Himesh's number.'

Meanwhile, Shilpa's film career continued. The latest release was *Shaadi Karke Phas Gaya Yaar*, again with Salman Khan. 'It's a nice commercial film and has got a great script,' she said. 'I think the audiences are going to like it.'

The film had, in fact, been delayed in its release, something that had very much upset the other star, Salman. Shilpa was keen to back him up. 'In Salman's defence, I will say that he is one guy who has pushed this film till here,' she said. 'He put lots of energy and effort into this project and he is the most affected due to the delay in release.'

As for Shilpa herself, she was adamant she was not concerned about what was next. 'It has been almost 13 years and I never needed to think about my future in advance,' she remarked. 'I never planned anything. I never thought I would last so long in the industry. The work kept coming my way. I have done a variety of roles – comedy, romance, thriller, offbeat, everything. In my forthcoming films, the audience will see me in a completely new role. I am doing *Apne* and *Metro*. Both are commercial films and I am playing different kinds of roles in them.'

As for matrimony: 'Of course,' said Shilpa, 'I plan to settle down. I am waiting for the right person. The day I find someone, I will make a formal announcement.'

Poor Shilpa. No matter what else she did, the focus continued to be on her private life.

But her new show was to have far greater ramifications than even she could have imagined; her exposure on Indian television came at exactly the same time the producers of the celebrity version of *Big Brother* were just beginning to think who they were going to add to that year's mix. With every season of the show that passed, the audience expected something increasingly new and different to keep them entertained and, this time round, Endemol was considering adding someone altogether more exotic to the mix. After all, they'd already had the non-celeb celeb – Chantelle

Houghton – so what better this year than to look far overseas for their next candidate instead?

Shilpa, of course, had no idea what an unexpected turn her life was about to take. Rather, she was getting on with work as normal, continuing to build up her career. At times she must have wondered if it was all worth it. Whatever she did managed to have a downside as well as an up: for every film success, there'd been quite a few that hadn't done so well, and for every television triumph there was carping in the background that this was, after all, TV and not the silver screen, and wasn't that a bit of a comedown after such early promise?

Being the professional that she was, Shilpa simply got on with it. She'd never complained about any career problems in the past and she wasn't about to start now. Nor did she ever show any irritation about something else that was now constantly raising its head: namely, comparisons with her sister Shamita. This had been inevitable ever since Shamita had become an actress in her own right, but Shilpa took it all with remarkably good grace.

Shamita, said Shilpa, was a remarkably hardworking actress. Like her sister, Shamita was put under a good deal of scrutiny where her figure was concerned, to the extent that Shilpa even had to speak out to defend her. Shamita's first film was *Mohabbatein* and, while there were rumours that she'd been a very gawky girl when she was signed up, her elder sister was happy to put these to rest. 'When Adi [Aditya Chopra] signed her on, he gave her three months to put on weight,' said Shilpa. 'Look at her in *Mohabbatein* – she has the most toned body. You can't get that in three months. I think she is very focused and hardworking.'

Indeed, like her older sister, Shamita had not originally set out to be a film star. 'To tell you the truth, Shamita didn't want a film career,' said Shilpa. 'She has a diploma in fashion designing. But when Yashji offered her the film through Karan [*Johar*], Manish [Malhotra] and our friends, we thought she couldn't get a better launch film. Yashji is someone I always admired. We knew that, whatever the end product, it would be fabulous. So she might as well be part of a film in which she would be appreciated than work in a flop film. As it turned out, it was the right move. *Mohabbatein* has turned out a winner. Shamita has signed on for a few films, but I'd rather let her speak about them.'

Like her sister, Shamita soon had to contend with talk that all was not going as well in her career as it could have done. Shilpa was rather irritated by this. 'I don't agree, I think she's doing fine for herself,' she said, when this was put to her. 'Her acting skills have been appreciated, which I think is positive news.'

And what of the constant comparisons with Shilpa? 'But that's inevitable,' said Shilpa. 'I'm always willing to stand by Shamita. I know she will make it. I may do everything for her but, when it comes to acting, she has to do it herself. Even if I may like to, I cannot act for her.'

Then there were Shilpa's other commitments. *Big Brother* was actually not her first brush with British television, as, in February 2006, she participated in a BBC World Service Trust television programme designed to raise awareness of AIDS in India. It had, after all, been a cause close to her heart ever since she'd starred in *Phir Milenge*.

She was not the only Bollywood celebrity involved: others were Viveik Oberoi, Dia Mirza and Raveena Tandon. Partners in the project included India's National AIDS Control Organisation and Doordarshan TV, and Shilpa was delighted to be taking part. 'I have participated to show my solidarity to people living with HIV-AIDS. I will do anything for them to feel wanted and special,' she said, at the launch for the programme in Delhi.

The show – also a reality show – was called *Haath Se Haath Milaa* [Let's Join Hands] and, in each episode, a Bollywood star joins a young achiever whose work involves raising awareness about HIV-AIDS. Others taking part included Tabu, Fardeen Khan, John Abraham, Bipasha Basu, Abshishek Bachchan and Sunil Shetty. 'The Bollywood factor is there to entertain – to get us eyeballs, but also to be inspirational and aspirational for viewers,' said the project's creative director Anu Malhotra.

By this time, Shilpa's appeal had spread to the extent that United Spirits also signed her up as the brand ambassador for its vodka brand, Romanov. Her glamorous appeal was exactly what the company wanted, and did no harm at all in getting her name better known overseas.

'United Spirits is committed to achieving a leadership position in the Indian and international vodka market,' said Mr Lala, the company's president. 'As a part of our brand-building initiative, the company is partnering with Bollywood actress Shilpa Shetty as the brand ambassador for Romanov. Shilpa is an aspirational icon. Her innate style, energy and attitude highlight the core attributes of the brand. We will use her mass appeal to herald an enhanced customer experience.'

Shilpa was equally pleased. 'It is a pleasure to be associated with UB, which is the industry leader today,' she said. 'I look forward to partnering with Romanov. I vibe really well with the brand's youthful attitude. The brand is definitely going places and I wish it all the very best. Now we will grow together.'

That was an understatement. Shilpa had established herself internationally, but her biggest challenge to date was still to come. For negotiations had been going on behind the scenes for some time now for a daring new departure, one that had never been tried out before on British reality TV. In a bid to gain further international recognition, Shilpa was looking for new challenges, and she certainly got that. No one could have imagined what was about to happen, but she was about to find herself at the centre of a controversy that would spread right across the world.

14

She Who Laughs Last

In many ways, it made absolute sense, for the link between Britain and India is an old one: ever since the Empire, there has been a mutual fascination between the two countries, and what better idea to combine elements and see how they mixed together on live TV? The fact that some of the British element rather let the side down and that the whole thing turned into a class conflict is something that couldn't have been forecast at the earliest stages.

It was actually the press in India who first picked up on what was going on. At the beginning of January 2007, the following post appeared on Bollywoodblog.com: 'Reality Television is taking on

Bollywood and some of the biggest names in tinseltown, Kareena Kapoor, Shilpa Shetty, Malaika Arora Khan and Lara Dutta are the top contenders for the famous show *Big Brother*. Global Reality TV Leader Endemol was in Mumbai and has shot promos with the Bollywood babes at Gateway of India and other famous Mumbai tourist spots.

'While Malaika and Shilpa have both been active on television with dance-based reality shows *Nach Baliye* (on Star One) and *Jhalak Dikhla Jaa* (on Sony TV) respectively, it is a big chance for Kareena and Lara to make their TV debut. *Big Brother* is a reality-based show, where about twelve contestants live in a specially designed house totally disconnected from the outside world. They are all alone ... except for the millions of viewers watching them. The participants try to avoid periodic publicly voted evictions and win a cash prize.

'Kareena and Lara, both have "date-n-mate" problems, as beaus Shahid and Kelly are not too excited about the fact, so that leaves Malaika and Shilpa as the front runners.

'So will it be the "Chaiyya Chaiyya" or the "Chura Ke Dil Mera" gal on *Big Brother*? We'll have to wait and watch.'

In fact, the ultimate contest between Shilpa and Jade

was to prove far more engrossing than anyone could possibly have expected, while Shilpa herself had no idea what was about to come her way. As she herself put it, British reality television was to prove nothing like anything she'd experienced before, not simply courtesy of the crass behaviour of some of the inmates, but also because the show ended up causing an international row.

Indeed, the ramifications turned out to be extraordinary. Almost the first thing that happened as soon as Shilpa left the house was that the British Prime Minister requested to meet her. 'It's a huge honour,' said Shilpa, who must have been wondering how on earth all this came about. 'I am humbled. The row has been politicised but why wouldn't I want to meet Tony Blair? I would meet with anyone who wants to meet me and who has shown solidarity.'

It was becoming clear – she wasn't having an audience with him, it was the other way round.

Nor was that all: Shilpa was even set to meet the Queen after receiving an official invite to attend a reception at Marlborough House in London to celebrate Commonwealth Day on 12 March 2007. And then, of course, came the news that Jade was checking into rehab, something Shilpa handled with her customary grace. 'I have respect for her,' she said. 'She is taking it seriously and I know that she has done it for her children rather than showing off to the world. I know Jade that much.'

To her great credit, Shilpa was also very shocked to see Jo's appearance on GMTV, in which she broke down entirely. 'Jo looks shattered,' said Shilpa. 'My heart goes out to her. I feel terrible. We did connect on some level, there is no rancour and hate is such a horrible word. I feel sorry for what she and Jade are going through. It was very juvenile bullying. It was like being in school but I don't think they would say the same things today.'

The traumas apart, Shilpa believed that taking part was 'the most courageous and difficult thing I have ever done in my life. I was away from home, in a different country with a different culture, where I wasn't known as a celebrity,' she explained to the *Mirror* newspaper. 'I signed the contract two days before I flew – it happened so suddenly. It was the first time I had travelled alone.'

And would she do it again? 'No way,' said an adamant Shilpa. 'I was shocked by the lack of respect, the burping, farting, drinking and swearing. Great Britain is where Shakespeare was from – it's known for its culture and high tea but I didn't see any of that, apart from Cleo. I was never controlling, I just wanted to go with the flow. There was never a time when I said, "You have to do it my way." When Jade said I was spending too much time in the kitchen, I took a back seat. I like to defuse trouble. [But] I don't regret it for a single millisecond. It has given me so much. It's just the beginning. I'm knackered right now. I just need to get some sleep and I want to unwind. All the creative decisions are taken by me and all the financial ones by my mother. I don't even know how much I make. I'm so blasé about money.'

She certainly hadn't lost her sense of humour, though: soon after coming out of the house, and debating her various career options, she commented, 'I'd love to do a cookery show called *If Shilpa Can, Anyone Can*. Or maybe I should do an advert for chicken Oxo cubes.'

Whatever was next on the cards, though, she was getting ready to take full advantage of all the opportunities open to her. 'My visa has been extended and I am going to stay in the UK for a bit,' she said.

The visit to the House of Commons, when it came about, very nearly turned into a riot, like so much that Shilpa touched in her post-*Big Brother* existence. With the Labour MP Keith Vaz as her host, and wearing a white sari and a garland around her neck that had been presented to her by Vaz's nine-year-old daughter, Anjali, she went to the House of Commons to watch Prime Minister's Questions, before having lunch with a group of besotted admirers and meeting Tony Blair himself. There was near uproar, much to the displeasure of parliamentary figures, who were unhappy about the chaos caused by the visit. No matter: nothing could dampen the spirits of those present.

Of PM's Questions itself, Shilpa rather undiplomatically revealed, 'I thought it'd be really boring, but I quite enjoyed it,' before going on to rule out going into politics in India when she got back. (Matters really were getting slightly ridiculous at this stage.) 'I've never really been politically inclined,' Shilpa explained. 'Nobody has spoken to me about joining any party.'

And again, of course, she was asked about her tormentors on *Big Brother*. 'I have forgiven them and I have moved on and I request that the media moves on,' she said firmly.

He was 'very, very sweet' Shilpa revealed, mentioning that the PM gave her a painting of the Commons signed by himself and Cherie. 'He said I carried myself with utmost dignity and that he was sorry for what I went through in the [*Big Brother*] house.'

Nor were Messrs Blair and Vaz the only politicians to bask in the aura of Shilpa's glamour. The Culture Secretary Tessa Jowell managed to shoulder her way in to give her a gift, while Hazel Blears, Labour Party chairman, uttered, 'You look so glamorous.' Jack Straw managed to find the time to have his picture taken with her and MPs of all parties crowded around the table where she was having lunch. The menu was divulged to the starstruck, who learned she'd had smoked salmon, chicken – oh, the irony! – and something called Shilpa's delight, an array of desserts prepared by the Commons chefs.

As interest in Shilpa grew, so did speculation about a possible marriage partner. Her spokesman in India, Dale Bhagwagar, laughed it off. 'Right now, the world wants to marry Shilpa, but it depends on Shilpa who she wants to marry,' he said. 'Sunandaji [Shilpa's mother] did say in jest to a couple of foreign scribes that she hopes to find an NRI [Non-resident Indian] groom for Shilpa, but that statement shouldn't be taken literally. Shilpa is a clever, smart and intelligent girl and ultimately she will definitely get the right guy for herself.

'I wonder why the media is always in a tearing hurry to marry her off. Let the girl chase her dreams. After *Celebrity Big Brother*, let her enjoy the success and grow in life and then, who knows, one day her Prince Charming might just walk into her life. At the moment, it's movies and work that encompasses her dreams. She is at a very interesting stage in her career where she's got the world looking up to her. Like I wish to become the biggest and richest publicist in the world, I also wish Shilpa to become the biggest and richest actress in the world. What's wrong in earning more and more and being rich? We all strive for the same, don't we?'

But she was clearly going to be more than just a pretty face. Shilpa fever seemed to grow with every day that she was out of the house, with organisations everywhere clamouring to get a piece of the action. The latest to step in was the charity Act Against Bullying, who signed her up as a supporter. 'The way she handled the bullying on television makes her the perfect role model,' said Louise Burfitt-Dons, a spokeswoman for the charity. 'She came out on top after behaving with dignity and poise, and her ordeal highlights the need to ensure children are taught manners and the importance of not offending people.'

Offers continued to flood in. BBC's *Question Time*

asked Shilpa to appear on its panel – its host, David Dimbleby, said that the topic of Shilpa's bullying had provoked more e-mails than any subject in the past. The number of complaints about the show continued to soar, at the time of writing reaching 55,000. A tongue-in-cheek article appeared in the *Observer* newspaper, accusing Shilpa of bullying the nation while at the same time providing indispensable guidance on style tips.

And she had certainly done that. One of the reasons Shilpa had proved so enormously popular with the public was that not only did she display grace and forgiveness, but that she was a looker, too. Everything she wore had been commented on from the moment she entered the *Big Brother* household, and her appearance continued to cause almost as much comment as the great bullying row. Indeed, there seemed to be two main topics people wanted to ask Shilpa about: how had she felt when she was bullied, and just how did she manage to look like that? She was happy to pass on her style secrets.

'Don't overaccessorise,' she told the *Mirror*. 'Wear big earrings but nothing on your neck, just some bangles or an amulet. I would like to do a line of those.

'Pick one item of clothing that's striking and keep

everything else understated. Many people throw loud items together like a shimmery top, shiny trousers and metallic shoes – big mistake!

'Never follow trends or slavishly buy from the designer in favour, but pick what emphasises your body. And always match your belt with your shoes and bag.' (This last, incidentally, was the kind of style advice that British women had been given in the mid-20th century – yet another example of Shilpa, be it in her grooming or her behaviour, harking back to a more civilised era of British society.)

'Develop your own style,' she continued. 'Beyonce has her own distinct look and Victoria Beckham always looks smart and chic. Among the housemates, Danielle had a young, frivolous sense of style and Cleo was always classy. My basic rule is "less is more". Wearing a heavy base, caked powder and red rouge just looks scary.

'Never do your face in public. You distort your face to apply cosmetics and that is not an attractive look, which is why I applied mine away from the cameras in the *Big Brother* bathroom.

'Accentuate just one feature. If, like me, you want to draw attention to your eyes, keep your lipstick quite understated. If you have lovely, pouty lips, wear a darker gloss and keep your eyes subtle. Eyelash curlers can open up your eyes and give them definition without the need for layers of mascara. Use false eyelashes for a more glamorous night-time look.

'No matter how late I come home, I always remove my make-up. I mix pure coconut oil with olive oil, smooth it over my skin and wipe it off with cotton wool. It's naturally soothing to skin.

'Try to sleep for a minimum of eight hours a day and never use soap on your face – it's too harsh. Don't overload your skin with fancy products. My mum, who is 57 and has amazing skin, says the more you use when you're young, the worse it gets when you age. And try having your eyebrows threaded at a salon to avoid in-growing hairs.'

It was all excellent advice, and yet what continued to fascinate the most was Shilpa herself. Her admirers could be found everywhere, not just in front of the television screen, or indeed, the House of Commons. A priest, Friar Frank McManus – who celebrated mass at St Joseph's Church, The Rock in Ballyshannon – held Shilpa up as an example to be followed to a group of sixth-formers, commenting on her modest clothing and the fact that she seemed to speak English better than anyone else on the show. With spectacular timing, *OK!*

magazine had announced it was to launch in India some months back: it goes without saying who its first cover star was.

And then there was marriage, marriage, marriage ... When she was in the *Big Brother* house, Shilpa allowed her e-mail address to be made public without any idea of the response she would get. What happened was what everybody already knew: the whole world wanted to marry Shilpa – or to put it slightly more accurately, she received thousands of marriage proposals. Even so, none was to be the right man.

She was greatly amused by all this. 'The response has been overwhelming,' she said. 'I am very touched and extremely moved by it, but I want to tell all the people out there that my e-mail address is not a marital portal. I am someone who believes that we are who we are because of our audiences and, although I am not computer savvy at all, I said let's do it,' she said of the decision to make the address public. 'I'm told some of the proposals are really funny but I just haven't had a chance to see them for myself because of my busy work schedule. I really don't know when I will get married and, to be honest, I haven't found the perfect man yet.'

Where would it all end? Wherever Shilpa wanted it to seemed to be the answer. With every day that passed, new opportunities arrived, new invitations flooded in – the Shilpa show was well and truly established as the only place to be seen in town.

It has been an extraordinary story: Shilpa is the first ever Bollywood star to become a household name in the West. Others have made their mark on Western consciousness, but never like this, and never so quickly before now. Not only had Shilpa won out over the other housemates, she had also proved wrong those in Bollywood who said she was making a big mistake in going on to the show and that her career was all but over. If interest in Shilpa continues at the current rate, she will last a good many more years.

Shilpa's new friend Ian, from the *Big Brother* household, had also got caught up in it all. 'It was madness,' he said, of his exit from the house. 'Because I didn't know what I was coming out to, it was very, very strange. I took Shilpa shopping in Selfridges a couple of days back and that was madness. I'm going round for a Chinese next week.'

Lucky Ian, to be allowed to be her friend.

This really was a unique happening in the annals of British television: never had a show produced such an unexpected result and never had an individual been catapulted overnight from Bollywood babe to international peace icon. Shilpa seemed torn between amusement and bemusement; she was clearly as taken aback as anyone else by what had happened, but was certainly not about to let an opportunity like this pass her by.

Nor could she have thought that all the years of endeavour in Bollywood would end in this; that she might well be an underrated actress who deserved far more kudos than she'd ever got – and yet what finally provided her with international recognition was a British reality-television show. The late John Lennon once observed, 'Life is what happens while you're making other plans.' Rarely can a story have illustrated this as much as Shilpa's had done to date.

But it was not just Shilpa who was to benefit from her experiences in the *Big Brother* household: far from it. There were a good many winners from this particular series – and a good few more to come.

15
And the Winner Is ...
(Part II)

As the dust began to settle on Britain's biggest televisual furore in years, it did seem that most of the people involved had achieved their objective. Shilpa, for a start, had gone from being a complete unknown in the West to prospective Bond girl, such was the international interest people were now beginning to show. Her advisers were salivating at the prospect.

'Shilpa loves challenges and stunts,' said her publicist Dale Bhagwagar, shortly before she was announced the winner. 'She is a perfect package of looks, figure, talent and intellect. If her mind-blowing action sequences in last year's Bollywood movie *Dus*

are anything to go by, she is no less than India's answer
to Lara Croft. Hollywood film offers have started
coming in. Apart from the US and Britain, offers are
coming from Spain and Singapore too. Also, the
Indian film industry suddenly seems to have woken up
to the new Shilpa … She is leading all the betting sites
[about the outcome of *Big Brother*]. The racist slurs
have stirred people's emotion. For us, Shilpa is just
front-page news but in Britain she is more than news.
Shilpa is feelings, emotions and much more. I am
expecting nothing less than a win from Shilpa. I hope
glory will be hers.'

Even before she left the house, offers of mega deals
were already starting to pour in. There was the
possibility that she might front the reality show *Cricket
Star*, an Indian version of which has already been a
great success. The fee mentioned for that alone was
£100,000, and the show's chief executive Fraser
Castellino has described her as the 'perfect host'.

Another possibility is the lead role in a BBC comedy
set in an Indian call centre. One of the show's writers is
Sanjeev Bhaskar, best known for *The Kumars at No.
42*, and he visited Mumbai at around the time Shilpa
left the house to see if she would be interested. 'She
would be perfect for the show,' he said. 'If she is keen,

I will write her a part. She has shown she appeals to the British viewing public and that cannot be ignored now by screenwriters back in London.'

The other writers on the show are two of the most successful small-screen artists in Britain: Maurice Gran and Laurence Marks, who were responsible for, among much else, *Birds of a Feather* (1987–1997), *Goodnight Sweetheart* (1993–1999) and *Love Hurts* (1992–1994). 'Shilpa Shetty has maintained poise, grace and compassion in the house,' Sanjeev continued.

'She has acted as a young, well-brought-up modern Indian and has ironically presented traits that most people outside of India consider to be traditional British values. All of this in the face of sustained snide and adolescent attitudes from some of her housemates; she needs to be congratulated. If there is another series of *The Kumars*, then she would be most welcome at No. 42, although I think she would be an interesting guest at the call centre if the project goes to series.'

According to Shamita, Shilpa might well be tempted to go to No. 42. 'She and I are great fans of the Kumars,' she revealed. 'We watch it each time it's on Indian television and it makes us laugh a great deal.'

In fact, the world is now Shilpa's oyster. Any number of lucrative advertising and promotional deals could now be in the pipeline, in India and in the West. 'Shilpa has become the face of the new India,' said Nirvik Singh of *Grey Global*, one of the world's biggest advertising companies. 'She did not crack in the *Big Brother* house. She could get half a million pounds if she did get the deal right.'

British-based PR executive Mark Borkowski concurred: 'Shilpa has got a huge career ... She handles herself well, she's highly intelligent,' he said. 'The British Asian audience is a valuable audience for companies to plunder.'

Shilpa herself was quite overwhelmed at the difference in her life before and after life in the *Big Brother* house. 'It's a new high, new phase and a new life for me,' she said. 'Earlier, I was only recognised by the Asian community, but now to be chased by the paparazzi and to be acknowledged by the Britishers is a strange feeling. Recently, when I walked the red carpet for a film première, the crowd screamed as I stepped out. I was choked with emotion.'

Even before he was hired, that old PR professional Max Clifford was in no doubt that Shilpa was poised to profit massively from the show, as would others through her help. 'The programme has raised the spectre of racism, bullying and cultural ignorance –

Shilpa could do a lot through her public persona to heal and mediate around those issues,' he remarked.

The whole show has certainly transformed her career prospects in India. 'I don't think Shilpa Shetty is passé any more,' said Suneel Darshan, who worked with Shilpa on *Jaanwar*. 'Her participation and presence on the international show has been very effective in bringing out an issue that has been so often placed under the cover. My respect for her as a woman of calibre and substance has definitely increased, so has my entire perception of her as a person. I have now begun to see her as a great combination of beauty and brains. Besides, she's been looking fabulous on the show. It has given a big boost to her image, no doubt.'

Director Madhur Bhandarkar agreed. 'The kind of opposition and problem that Shilpa encountered does happen on reality shows because there's pent-up anger and a sense of one-upmanship,' he said. 'Moreover, it has become a fashion to use abusive language against Indians but the way she tackled the situation speaks a lot of her intelligence. Her image as an actress and the way she is perceived has definitely changed. I am definitely impressed with her.'

Director Tanuja Chandra thinks the whole issue might have been overblown, but she, too, feels that

Shilpa stands to gain a lot. 'I don't think the issue demanded so much attention as to necessitate the intervention of big political personalities like Tony Blair but the attention that Shilpa has got out of the show has certainly served the purpose of her participating in it,' she said. 'She should now aim to win the game as far as possible. One thing is for sure, it will certainly not take away from her popularity – on the contrary it has only added to her career prospects. This was the right step at the right time in her career.'

As for Channel 4, if anyone really thinks it has been damaged by the controversy, that person cannot understand television in Britain today. Just days after various executives discussed the ramifications of the programme with the board, Kevin Lygo, Channel 4's director of television, let slip what he actually thought about the row.

Bosses were worried as the 2007 show threatened to turn into the most boring *Big Brother* ever. And, as we all now know, Jade and her accomplices rescued it from that fate. 'Let's put this in perspective – this was in danger of being the most boring *BB* that we'd had in many years and we were thinking, "Oh dear, what can we do?"' he said. 'And then suddenly, from the cooking of a chicken going wrong, this argument erupted and then was taken on by the media and then erupted into this extraordinary story. I think the programme was produced and managed very well. I think we made the right decisions all the time.'

It was a 'fantastic thing' it prompted such debate, he said, even provoking a motion in the House of Lords.

Had he ever considered handing in his resignation about the furore? 'Not in the slightest,' he said, nor were any other jobs on the line. The priority now was to re-establish links with Carphone Warehouse.

Not everyone was quite so sanguine. 'They are living in cloud-cuckoo land,' Tory MP Anne Widdecombe commented. 'There were a record number of complaints and those complaints came from people who were actually watching it. Of course they had a ratings boost. But, if they think that is going to do the programme much good in the longer term, I doubt it very much.'

Trevor Phillips, chairman for the Commission of Equality and Human Rights, was not impressed either. 'What we saw on *Big Brother* was racism. It was prejudice, and should have no place in our society ... what took place was a noxious brew of old-fashioned class conflict, straightforward bullying, ignorance and quite vicious racial bigotry.'

Time will tell what effect it will have. Morality and British television are frequently strangers to each other, and there is every possibility that *Big Brother* will actually secure a new lease of life after this.

Meanwhile, the debate about racism continues. Was what happened within the *Big Brother* walls racist and should it have been allowed to be screened? What it really seemed to amount to was a conflict over class and the gang mentality produced when a group of rather dim-witted girls was pitched against a bright and attractive one, with race as the weapon rather than the motive behind it all. 'I think this racism stuff has been taken out of perspective,' said Anil Dharker. 'Shilpa has not gone to London to represent India in the United Nations. She is in a reality-TV show and that is it.'

Honey Kalaria also believes the racism angle was overplayed. 'I think Jade was a very big bully; she was definitely a bully. But Shilpa handled it brilliantly,' she remarked. 'There was a petition going on about the racism side of things but I didn't sign it. I really felt right from the beginning it wasn't racism. I still feel that.'

As for Shilpa's dignified response, Honey felt her upbringing played a part, and that the Jades of this world are to be found everywhere. 'In Asian society, there is one thing that we are taught and that is how to sacrifice, how to be tolerant, how to be able to accept,' she revealed. 'These are values that parents instil in you. [But] You could equally have found an Asian person in the *Celebrity Big Brother* house who behaved badly. I just think that, for certain people, it's not really their fault, it's just their environment and how they've been brought up. They may not have the intelligence to be able to communicate.'

But the police, at least, are taking it all seriously. Danielle has, at her request, been interviewed by them, and, at the time of writing, it had just been reported that the same had happened to Shilpa. 'The police quizzed Shilpa on what went on in the *Big Brother* house,' said a source. 'They asked about her feelings when she was inside and now she is out. They also wanted to know if she thought her contract had been breached – and if she felt any of the attacks were racially motivated. The police told Shilpa they wanted to interview everyone in the house. And they wanted to interview bosses at Channel 4, but had not been able to yet.'

Jo O'Meara, meanwhile, has been, in her own words, 'devastated' by what has happened. She took a lot longer than the others to apologise and has looked quite disbelieving about all that has happened. 'I feel, if this is what a TV show does to people, then it shouldn't be a TV show,' she said. 'The whole thing has been so unfair and so cruel. I've not been portrayed as the person I really am.

'I don't think you can get much lower. They say you have to hit rock bottom before you can build yourself up. I just hope I'm at the bottom now. I'm not a racist person, I never, ever have been. None of it makes sense. I don't know how this has all happened.'

Meanwhile, the police have extended their inquiry into potential racist abuse by demanding unseen footage from Channel 4, in which it was alleged Shilpa was called a 'Paki'. Channel 4 was not forthcoming.

'We are in an ongoing dialogue with the police and have already provided them with access to many hours of broadcast programmes,' said a Channel 4 spokeswoman. 'The police have now requested untransmitted programme material. Channel 4's policy, consistent with that of all broadcasters, is to require the police to obtain a court order before such material is handed over. The police must satisfy a court that such material is of substantial value to their investigation and that disclosure is in the public interest.'

At the time of writing, Hertfordshire Police are still

interviewing housemates and preparing a file which will be passed to the Crown Prosecution Service to decide whether or not to press charges.

As for poor Jade – and it *is* possible to feel a certain amount of pity for her – Shilpa's family urged forgiveness. 'There is so much being said about this young woman that can only deeply hurt her,' said Surendra. 'She said a few hurtful words towards my daughter, but that should not also make her the victim of aggression and hate. We are Hindus who pray for peace. My family follows the Mahatma Gandhi's principle of non-violence and non-animosity towards others. Perhaps Shilpa is unaware at this time of much of what was said about her, but, when she comes to know, it won't mean much to her. I am absolutely overwhelmed with the love and support that has been shown by the UK public towards Shilpa. A few distasteful remarks by a few individuals do not mean the whole country is bad.'

Even Shilpa, however, had her limits, saying she would not be taking part in a programme to help revive Jade's career. 'I am no Samaritan – I'm just human,' she said. 'If anybody thinks I can resurrect somebody's career or character, they're wrong, it's just not possible for me to do. If I need to speak to Jade, I don't need to do it as a publicity stunt – I'll do it in private, between ourselves.'

She also expressed surprise about Jade's apology. 'I didn't expect it,' she said. 'It was very unlike Jade to apologise. Maybe *CBB* had asked her about it and it dawned on her.'

Nor, she said, had she snubbed a wrap party, saying she hadn't been invited. 'I knew nothing about the party,' she revealed. 'I did not snub it, I didn't get an invite. Perhaps they didn't know how to contact me.'

Other than Shilpa herself, the biggest winner from the series has to be the agent – some would say 'super-agent' – John Noel. Originally Davina McCall's agent, his association with *Big Brother* began when Davina became host of the show. With the advent of 'Nasty Nick' in the first series, John realised the potential for people who achieved celebrity merely by virtue of having appeared on television, and began signing up and fashioning careers for both the professionals and the amateurs who came his way.

He is now Jade's agent – 'I'll have a word with John,' she confided to Jo as the race row began to develop – as well as Pete Bennett and Chantelle Houghton. He also represents two more *Big Brother* presenters: Dermot O'Leary and Russell Brand, to say nothing of Cleo Rocos, leading some people to speculate that that connection is the reason why Cleo didn't step in to shut Jade up.

And, as Jade's agent, it was John who began to work fast behind the scenes to save her career. It was he who orchestrated her *mea culpa* interview with the *News Of The World*, he who made sure it was videotaped so that everyone could see Jade sobbing in contrition, he who ensured Jade's fee for the interview – and for *Big Brother* – went to charity, and he who then orchestrated her march around the nation's television studios begging forgiveness from the nation. His fellow agents can only watch him in awe.

'My reputation in the business is I'm gruff, which I always thought was quite funny. I can be bad-tempered and let off steam, and if something is written that's not true I say so, and some people don't like that,' he says.

Of his stupendous success in turning non-entities into celebrities, he continued, 'What became apparent to me was the housemates had a battery life. When they come out of the house, that begins to run out. If you can find a way of recharging it, that's the key.'

This strategy has, above all, worked exceptionally well for Jade, whose very existence has now been turned into a highly profitable soap opera.

Other agents are fulsome in their praise. 'He is like

the medieval science of alchemy in that he is good at turning shit into gold. He's absolutely brilliant, given the clients he has, like Jade,' says Alex Armitage, who represents Jeremy Vine and Sir David Frost.

Another source said, 'When the contestants leave *Big Brother* they get taken away to a place in the country and John shows them all the covers of *Heat* he's got them. He can prove what he can do for them.'

And what he can do is to change their lives. This has led some people to say that, by virtue of the fact that he represents so many people who are connected to the programme, he has too much power over *Big Brother*, a charge he strongly refutes. 'I was looking at how we could cross-promote from *Big Brother*, and make the whole thing work for everybody,' he says mildly. 'Now I'm being criticised for representing more than one client involved in *Big Brother*.' Although not by the clients themselves, who have profited massively from the association.

And, of course, some of the other contestants benefited, too. Jermaine, who might have won had circumstances been different, proved himself to be an immensely affable and likeable man, a hit with the British public and someone who also might be spending more time in the future in the UK. 'Plans for a Jackson Five musical show are at an early stage but we are hoping to open it in a London theatre as soon as possible,' he said, the day after the series ended, as the dust began to clear. A positive outcome for him looked certain.

As for the biggest winner of all, it currently looks as if she need only name her project and it will be done. Her popularity with the British public is now such that crowds have been turning out in their thousands to see her – and, at the time of writing, the possibility has been mooted that she will star in a film opposite Hugh Grant, that most British of heartthrobs.

In February 2007, turning up to the première of Grant's most recent film, *Music and Lyrics*, with her mum in tow, Shilpa commented, 'I really love Hugh's movies and I really look forward to seeing this one.'

For a girl who seemed to be at the end of a Bollywood career, this is big news indeed. Faced with a choice between Hugh Grant and James Bond, could life get any better for Shilpa?

And given her first actions after granting an audience to the Prime Minister et al at the House of Commons, Shilpa certainly seems to have the common touch. Her first announcement was not a film project, but the launch of an AIDS charity to help AIDS victims in

India. Of course, this is a cause with which she has been associated for some time, but it is not putting it too strongly to say there are echoes of Princess Diana here – a very beautiful and glamorous woman helping those who are very much in need.

The launch took place in Leicester, in the Peepul Centre, where an absolute scrum turned out to greet her. 'It is a cause that has been very, very close to my heart,' said Shilpa. 'Not just now but for the last four years. India is the second-largest affected country in the world with AIDS so I think it's important to do something about it and it's every person's right to live with dignity in our country, even if it's a person who is HIV positive. It's very difficult to do that only because there's no awareness and I am going to do my bit to support that and I think starting this organisation is really going to help us try a new beginning.'

And what, finally, did the series of *Big Brother* really prove? That Britain is a racist nation? Almost certainly not, given that it was Shilpa, not Jade, who was the outright winner. The country rallied in support of her: indeed, if anything, what *Big Brother* proved this time round is that Britain still stands up for the person who is being put upon, whatever their skin colour, and whatever their background.

Shilpa took a huge gamble and it has paid off. That Princess Diana comparison is not a one-off. Ever since Diana's death in August 1997, the world has been on the lookout for a beautiful, glamorous woman capable of showing great compassion, both to individuals – Jade – and to a greater number of people in need. The world is badly in need of heroes and heroines, and if one, Diana, can be found in the unlikely reaches of the British aristocracy, then why should another not come from the Bollywood elite? He, or she, who dares wins, and Shilpa has certainly dared a lot.

Perhaps the greatest part of her story, though, is the illustration of the power of reality television. Almost unheard of a decade ago, it now has a power to shine a light not just on to individuals, but on society too. Endemol might have thought it was just creating something that might turn into compulsive viewing, but what it has actually done is to form a searchlight that can shine upon us all.

Of course, the only people who will really be able to benefit from that searchlight are the ones who have something to give back as well. And it is not too bold to say that Shilpa has shown Britain something this country has lost. Not only was she feminine and charming and slightly appalled by the ill-mannered habits of others present, she also presented a dignified aspect to the world that is not often seen in these days of lads and ladettes. Is it going too far to say that by her example she might actually change the face of British society? Certainly, this is a society that seems very much to want a change.

Whatever her longer-term influence, Shilpa has done herself and her country proud. Not once has she said anything unkind or cruel about the other contestants – or, indeed, about anyone else – not once has she shown any sort of cattiness or disagreeableness. She has earned what lies ahead. And, whatever that may be, Shilpa will rise to the occasion – perfectly groomed, beautifully coiffed and radiating goodwill towards everyone around her. Her mother, it seems, was right when she foresaw quite a future for her little baby, but even she can't have dreamed what that future would really look like. As it is, the future is Shilpa's – the new queen of reality TV.

Filmography

Life In A... Metro (May 2007) (Post-Production)

Apne (May 2007) (Under Production)

Durbar (2007) (To Go On Floor)
Inspector Barsaat Devi

Kahin Aag Na Lag Jaaye (2007) (On Hold)

Kaanch – The Broken Glass (2007) (Post-Production)

Shaadi Karke Phas Gaya Yaar (August 2006)
Ahana

Dus (July 2005)
Aditi

Fareb (July 2005)
Neha

Khamosh – Khauff Ki Raat (April 2005)
Sonia

Phir Milenge (August 2004)
Tamanna Sahni

Garv(July 2004)
Jannat

Darna Mana Hai (July 2003)
Gayathri

Junoon (2003)

Rishtey (December 2002)
Vaijanti

Karz – The Burden of Truth (December 2002)
Sapna

Hathyar (October 2002)
Gauri Shivalkar

Chor Machaye Shor (August 2002)
Kajal

Badhaai Ho Badhaai (June 2002)
Radha/Banto Betty

Indian (October 2001)
Anjali

Dhadkan (August 2000)
Anjali

Jung (2000)
Tara (Balli's Girlfriend)

Tarkieb (2000)
Preeti Sharma

Jaanwar (December 1999)
Mamta

Shool (November 1999)

Dancer (In Song 'UP Bihar')

Lal Baadshah (March 1999)
Lawyer's Daughter

Pardesi Babu (November 1998)
Chinni Malhotra

Aakrosh: Cyclone of Anger (April 1998)
Komal

Prithvi (August 1997)
Neha

Insaaf (May 1997)
Divya

Zameer (May 1997)
Roma

Auzaar (February 1997)
Prathna Thakur

Chhote Sarkar (November 1996)
Inspector Seema

Himmat (January 1996)
Nisha

Gambler (December 1995)
Ritu

Hathkadi (March 1995)
Neha

Aao Pyar Karen (November 1994)
Chhaya

Main Khiladi Tu Anadi (September 1994)
Mona/Basanti

Aag (August 1994)
Bijli

Baazigar (November 1993)
Seema Chopra